MW01504180

Old But Strong

The Journals

By Ian Duckett

For Molly and Louis

You did an awesome job Louise, two very happy wonderful kids that are so
bright, full of energy and love for live

All I do is do my best for them every day with always you in mind

Two wonderful kids I could not be more proud of
Love you always

Dad xx

Acknowledgements

Joanne Todd (Jo)
For the complete layout of this book

Russell Clark
Book cover, and photos within @studioportraiture

Other photos from the past, acknowledged on page

Training partners over the years, thank you for sharing the journey

Special thank you to Jon Torn, Paul Twig, Gary Thornton, Andrew Barber, Robin Gorry, Chris McHugh, Martin Shippin, Jo Todd, Debbie Scholefield, Vince Kerr, Philip Guy, Martin Wilson, Vince Sykes, Ian Cooper, Mark Jackson, Ian Prince

For being awesome training partners through the featured years in this book

Chris being there through all of them.

Thank you and love to you all

Last but not least, all my love to Jo,
for her love, support, and strength through everything

Ian xx

All rights reserved

Copyright BodyIndesign 2020

No part of this book may be reproduced in any form without written permission from Ian Duckett

This book is presented for information purposes only

Ian Duckett and BodyIndesign assume no responsibility in the correct use or incorrect use of the information within

Always consult your doctor

Contents

INTRODUCTION

This journal covers some great workout and eating structures that could help you immensely.

There is so much crap out there that confuses the trainer. How should I eat? What is the best workout for size, condition, and fitness?

The truth is there is no set pattern, routine, or eating plan.

You have got to find out what works for you. How do you do that?

Well that's easy you try programs and monitor the progress you make or lack of.

How do you feel? Is the food you are eating making you feel awesome – full of energy, lean and strong or not?

All this comes from just trying something and making notes.

My journals here will show you that even after 42 years of training and eating all the while keeping journals, I am still learning and experimenting, always – why?

Because as you age - you need to remain fluid and adaptable to everything that you do. Plus, it would be boring as hell if you knew it all and all this was a piece of piss.

So you will see, programs tried and tested, programs abandoned as I felt they were not right and brought on over-training. You will see nutrition tried and tested, and recipes made and rated. This will give you years' worth of information to try and adapt as your own.

As a starting point to this journal I want to give you the past 6 months or so in a nutshell – the programs that I/we did up to this point, along with the eating plans. This will bring you up to speed so to speak and allow the rest of the book/journal to flow for you.

This was a base program for the tail end of 2019 covering the two photo shoots I had done. Photos within and on the cover. It was a 2-day all body program. All body each time, but different moves each session. Workout A and B rotated over 3 days a week training; Tuesday, Thursday and Saturday.

Workout A

Rack shoulder press 1 set of 12

Squat to pins, set at parallel 1 set of 5

Back off set of squats 1 set of 12

Bench press 1 set of 5

Back off set of bench 1 set of 12

Curls thick bar 2 sets of 6

Sit ups on a high incline 2 sets of 10, weighted

Workout B

Light squat 1 set of 12

Deadlift 1 set of 5

Dumbbell bench press 1 set of 8

Weighted chins 1 set of 8

Dips 1 set of 8 to 10

Pushdowns 2 sets of 10 to 12

Calf raise 2 sets of 12

Notes

Whenever goal reps were made the weight was added up a few pounds. Sets were low and I only had a few non-taxing warm ups prior to my main set. This was a very good program that we will return to.

As you may note on some moves we did a base set of 5 for strength, and then a back off set of 12 or so for muscle stimulation.

The days went – Tuesday - Workout A, Thursday - Workout B, Saturday - Workout A, again, so you would have two of Workout A one week, and two Workout B the next. Odd times we would rest a day or so more if we felt we needed it.

Along with the program I walked/hiked an average of 60 miles a week. Only just prior to the photo shoot did I lower this to 30 miles a week to allow a little more fullness for the photo shoot.

Straight as I had done the photos I ramped up the hiking miles again.

Food was a baseline of around 3000 calories, and this kept me at 138lb to 140lb, in the shape I was in for the photos in this book.

Here is my baseline eating plan.

I even followed this whilst we were away in Gran Canaria very easily.

1. 3 eggs, bread, cheese, oats, honey with 2 liver tablets, 2 brewer's yeast and a vitamin C

2. Fruit and nuts

3. Bread with peanut butter, Greek yogurt, apple, 2 liver tablets, 2 brewer's yeast and a vitamin C

4. Protein bar, or fruit and nuts again

5. Tuna or fish, rice, vegetables, with 2 liver tablets, 2 brewer's yeast and a vitamin C.

6. Oats protein and nut butter

Supplements were desiccated liver – that I will explain later in the book, let's just say an awesome source of amino acids, minerals and iron. Brewer's yeast – very good for B vitamins for the digestion and utilisation of carbohydrates for energy.

I followed this diet but had the odd bar of organic chocolate as a break from it, or fish and chips now and then when we at the cabin. These cheats just kicked up my metabolism higher every time.

Upping the intensity

The next goal after the above program was to fill out a little more. Gain five or so pounds of fullness – which on my 5 ft 3 frame looks and feels much different. I was eating around 4000 calories a day or just over, and walking/hiking around 40 to 50 miles a week. I gained up to 149lb then as mentioned later in this book settled down to 145lb, and that felt much better for my goals.

As for building muscle I know nothing better in all the years I have trained as an all over body high intensity workout over 2 to 3 days. As you will see further in this book - I upped the intensity – i.e. pushed harder and increased the weight each week when my goal reps were achieved. I started to fill out and so did Jo. This is something again we will keep going back to as in the other program above.

Now you may ask why not stick to the same program and keep making gains? Well, you will only make gains for so long then your body will not give up anymore – so the programs need to change for you to keep progressing. The body adapts very quickly, and even more quickly the more years you have trained. I found that 6 to 8 weeks on a program is as much as you can milk a program for gains.

This program is based on the old nautilus type programs that were used and invented by Arthur Jones in the early 70s. I have had many a client as well as myself make awesome gains in this type of program.

Workout A

Squat 1 x 20

Bench press off the pins in the rack, bottom position 1 set of 8 to 10

Dips 1 set of 10

Chins 1 set of 8 to 10

Close grip bench 1 set of 8 to 10

Curls 1 set of 8 to 10

Sit ups 1 set of 15

Front neck work 1 x 20

Workout B

Rack press shoulders 1 set of 8 to 10

Deadlifts trap bar 1 set of 8 to 10

Stiff leg deadlifts 1 set of 8 to 10

Bent over rows 1 set of 8 to 10

Dumbbell chest press 1 set of 8 to 10

Dumbbell curl 1 set of 8 to 10

Triceps extensions 1 set of 15

Rear neck work 1 set of 20

As I pushed harder on this program we spread out the all body days of A and B, so Tuesday was A, Saturday was B, and Thursday we used as a weak point area day – just an easy day.

I did more calves, neck and abs, Jo did extra shoulders and arms.

The difference in this program to the other - is I took each main set to positive fail. Whereas in the other, it was a rep based program and not pushing too hard. Simply put, you increased the weight the next workout if you got your reps.

Diet was similar to the prior program but I just upped the volume of food and kept track of my calories. Increasing from 3000 baseline to over 4000 by a few hundred a week.

This brings us up to the present time and the programs and diet as such listed in this journal.

Enjoy and make gains, be healthy strong and fit.

Natural foods I eat, all organic

Tuna
Eggs – free range and fertile
Cottage cheese
Cheese
Goats milk
Nuts
Seeds
Fruits – and dried fruit
Vegetables and salad
Yogurt
Bread – rye and sour dough
Oats
Natural muesli
Honey
Rice – wholegrain
Potatoes
Berries
Chicken (only on rare occasions) - free range organic

I write out what I eat each day but no calorie counting. Eat for energy and health, body and strength will take care of itself.

Training moves

Chest

Bench
Incline Dumbbell Press
Flat Dumbbell Press
Dips
Incline Flyes
Flat Flyes
Crossovers

Back

Chins
Pulldowns
Rows
T-Bar Rows
Low Row
Deadlifts
½ Deadlift & Shrug

Legs

Squats
Leg Press
Hack Squats
Leg Extensions
Leg Curls
Stiff Leg Deadlifts
Sissy Squats
French Squats

Abs

Sit ups
Leg Raise
Side Crunch
Rope Crunch

Arms

Curls
Seated Dumbbell
Incline Dumbbell
Push Downs
Extensions
Overhead Rope Extensions
Bench Dips
Close Grip Rack Press

Shoulders

Rack Shoulder Press
Lat Raise
Bent Over Lat Raise
Standing Press
Upright Rows

Calves

Standing calf
Toe Press
Calf free on a block not machine

Winter 2020

Saturday 22 February 2020, 144

Power week, add up calories again for now.

<u>Training</u>

Rack bench press (4 holes up) first in gym top right rack, thick bar (thick bar weighs 47kg)	15kg a side x 12
	17.5kg a side x 10
	17.5kg, plus 1¼ a side x 8
	20kg a side x 6
	22.5kg a side x 3
Deadlifts	2 plates a side x 12
	2 plates plus 5kg a side x 10
	2 plates plus 10kg a side x 8
	2 plates plus 15kg a side x 6
	3 plates a side x 3
Bench press holds, 6 holes up, normal Olympic bar	120kg, for 10 seconds
	125kg, for 10 seconds
	130kg, for 10 seconds
Chins	No weight, 2 x 15
Sit ups high incline	10kg, 2 x 10

When a "bracket" is shown at the side of the moves, this means the moves are combined in either a super-set, tri-set, or giant-set.

Foods eaten

	Food	Supplements	Calories
1.	Eggs	Animal Pak	270
	Cheese		120
	Bagel		230
	Honey		100
2.	Pre workout oats		180
	½ scoop protein		100
3.	Pro after		280
4.	Sweet potato thing at Nandos – sweets at movies, Call Of The Wild – cheat meal		450
			600
5.	Tuna		200
	Rice		300
	Veg		50
	Oil		100
6.	Oats		360
	Protein		125
	Milk		240
	Raisins		
	Nut butter		3705

New program idea

Notes

Been messing about all week trying to get a hang on a program to suit our needs. Strong and fit and get show ready for girls, Jo and Debs.

1. Chest and back

2. Shoulders and arms

3. Legs

Over 3 days – one week power moves one week shape moves.

Power week

1. Rack bench press 12, 10, 8, 6, 3

   Jump set with... (jump sets are a slow super set – not rushed)

   Deadlifts 12, 10, 8, 6, 3

   Bench holds in rack 3 holds

   Chins 2 sets

2. Rack shoulder press 12, 10, 8, 6, 3

   Curls all 10 3 sets

   Close press all 10 3 sets

3. Calf raise 8 sets 15 reps 3 toe positions

   Squat 12, 10, 8, 6, 3

Shape week

Same body part split as above – but anything goes workouts, free style. Freestyle means – do as I feel is right at the time.

Train on instinct that day, just work hard, doing what comes to mind as the workout unfolds.

Sunday 23 February 2020

Rest day – only short walks

Total 6 miles, 2 a time

Yoga at bed for 20 mins

New diet idea - more Mediterranean style diet

Struggling with my belly at the moment too much food, again! Got to stop counting calories and eat when hungry and eat smaller amounts – be healthy!! Let weight settle.

Idea baseline plan

1. Eggs, 1 toast, yogurt and fruit
2. Fruit at gym if training
3. Fish and salad
4. Cheese plus fruit
5. Fish salad, or veg, and spud
6. Yogurt or cheese

Foods eaten

Food	Supplements
1. 1 eggs x 3, bread, muesli, goats milk	None today
2. Tuna, salad, cheese, oil	
3. Same as 2	
4. Granola and Greek yogurt	

Monday 24 February 2020, 145¼

Lots of short walks today maybe total of walks was around 6 miles, busy day at work.

Bedtime did 20 minutes of yoga and a little work on bad leg. I have a little wooden tool that I use to break up the scar tissue, it has worked wonders.

Foods eaten

Food	Supplements
1. 3 eggs, 1 slice sunflower bread, yogurt and an apple	Animal Pak
2. Goats cheese quiche that Sarah made, spud, veg and oil	
3. Tuna and rice, veg and oil	
4. Muesli and Greek yogurt	

My choice of gym

Most of the workouts here in this book at present time take place in a really old school gym called Dicky's Gym, right in the heart of a small town called Batley on the outskirts of Dewsbury, near Leeds. Which is why you will see some of the weights I record in my journal are in pounds as well as kgs.

It's a throwback to the 80s and has hardly changed much, since the owner Mark is as old school as they come. Somewhat like Micky in the Rocky movies – he's all business and hard work. Mark is actually a boxing trainer, training many of the country's pro-boxers, Josh Warrington to name a very prominent one.

So you can guess the gym's surroundings is seeped in the old boxing style gyms of the past – when you walk in it is actually like going back in time. I love that – it reminds me of the workouts of the past - the pain, sacrifice and glory of those days and you get serious. It's definitely not a fuck about and chat gym, there is hardly anybody in the weights section as it is predominantly a boxing gym, off to the side of the weights area. If there is someone else in the gym when we are in there they are definitely not on their phone.

I have owned many gyms in my time. I have trained in many gyms all over the world, and yes some have been awesome. But this gym is home.

It reminds me of my beginnings in this sport – how far I have come and how far I still want to go. My goals have changed as life goes on, they have to, you have to evolve or you will break and burn out. But I will never lose the feeling I have when I see and feel cold iron in my hands. The rattle of old plates on old school bars as I work on this never-ending never dying passion I have.

My two favourite places to train are Dicky's and my home gym, I treasure them both.

Tuesday 25 February 2020, 144½

Training

	Weight	Reps
Rack shoulder press	15kg a side	12
	16.5kg a side	10
	17.5kg	8
	17.5kg plus 1¼	6
	20kg a side	3
Curls thick bar	thick bar weighs 47kg	3 x 10
Close EZ bar press	26lb a side on this	2 x 10
Sit ups	Forced reps on last set used 10kg on forehead	2 x 20

Rack shoulder press is done in power rack 80 degree bench incline pressing off pins from a dead stop. Shoulders and upper chest.

Walked 5 miles later with 16lb pack, got in plenty of hills was jigged after – bit of yoga whilst watching TV later on.

Foods eaten

Food	**Supplements**
1. Eggs cheese veg	
2. Oats	
3. Pro after training	BCAA and C&G
4. Bread, pumpkin and rye – peanut butter, apple, yogurt	
5. Fruit, apple and banana	
6. Eggs boiled rice, cheat, bit of cake Sarah made	

C&G is creatine and glutamine, some I had left over, taken it only sporadically.

Wednesday 26 February 2020

Instead of walking today did a quick workout at home later on 19:00, normally train in a morning.

Training

Abs – Crunch, hypers, leg raise	20 each x 3 rounds
Incline dumbbell press Up and down rack	12, 10, 8, 6, 10
Chins wide grip	5 x 8
Lat raise up rack again, then down	5 x 12
One arm cross over, Changing each set – high – low – medium – range of motion across the body.	

Felt like doing a bit of training – nice night after work loved it, yoga then bed.

Trying to sort out food, think I have a bit of a bug Jo feels the same, feel like I am not digesting food well.

Foods eaten

Food

1. Pro, nut butter, banana, goats milk, honey, all blended
2. Same again – felt drinking calories would give my system a rest
3. Tuna, spuds, veg
4. Same as 3
5. Yogurt and Granola

Thursday 27 February 2020

Louise's day. Lou passed away 5 years ago today. Still think of her every day. Louis and I will go to the hospice and take flowers, chocolates and a card for the amazing staff up there at the Wakefield Hospice. Also flowers for Louise as she is still with us at home.

Later I walked 6 miles no weight added.

Foods eaten

Food

1. Pro as over page - blended
2. Bread, black rye. Cheese, nuts, apple, yogurt.
3. Rice, Tuna, cottage cheese, salad
4. Oats, pro, goats milk, nut butter

Friday 28 February 2020

Training – legs – shape week

* Should have been heavy! But this worked well as I was at home in-between clients

	Weight	Reps
Abs – crunch, leg raise, tucks		3 rounds 20 each
⌐ Leg extension	30kg	3 x 15
∟ Calf raise, different toe positions		3 x 20
⌐ Walking lunge,		3 x 24, 10kg each hand
∟ Calf raise, different toes		3 x 20
Machine squat (facing out)	50kg	3 x 10
Dumbbell squat, heels on plates, deep	10kg each hand	3 x 12

Foods eaten

	Food	Supplements	Calories
1	Try this out food wise today as if I am on trail		
	Before training – after walk		
	Big breakfast cooked or not		
	Oats	Animal Pak	360
	Raisins		140
	Pro		125
	Seeds		80
	Milk		80
	Dates		100
2.	After training and mid-morning		
	Nuts		200
	Fruit		160
	Milk	BCAA	80
3.	Nut ball, milk		440
4.	Nut ball, milk		440
5.	Tuna		150
	Oil		100
	Pasta		150
	Veg		100
	Bread		250
6.	Yogurt		250
	Total		3135

Saturday 29 February 2020, 144.5

Walk early

Shape week

Training

Movement	Weight	Reps
3 rounds of 4 exercises		
Sit ups		15
Leg raise		15
Side bends		15 each side
Hypers		15
Flyes	40lb	20, 15, 15
Pull downs	45kg	20
	50kg	15, 15
Bench press	50kg	15, 12, 12

Low rows	45kg	20
	50kg	15, 15
Dips	No weight	12, 12
Shrugs	150kg	15, 15

Foods eaten

	Foods	Supplements	Calories
1.	Breakfast		
	Oats		360
	Pro		125
	Raisins		140
	Nuts		200
	Milk		80
			905
2.	After training	BCAA	
	Fruit		160
3.	Fat ball (I made)		400
4.	Nuts		200
	Fruit		60
5.	Steak pie, spuds, peas at hotel		1000 (at a guess)
6.	Yogurt		200
		BCAA bed time	2925

At Whitby with Jo in hotel, awesome place.

Notes on nutrition – and hiking and training

- Within the first hour of exercise the body breaks down BCAA. When they are used up in the blood the body will break down tissue to burn

- Weights and high end aerobic exercise – uses mostly carbs

- Long term out-put at moderate levels eats up stored fat. But carbs are still used. Carbs still have to be present in glycogen storage. If used up – no fat will burn!! Lets' just say there has to be a mix carb fuel in the body for the body to tap into fat

- On long walks use maltodextrin in water. Glucose polymers. 30 – 60g per hour. Also take in (BCAA) regular to stop body tapping into tissue

- First – at the end of long hikes and training – hydrate! Plain water is okay at the days end. Then calories – large meals to restock the system, included protein, fats and carbs, good natural foods, and basic supplements

- Essentially this is what I am doing now with my food

Sunday 1 March 2020

Foods	Supplements
	BCAA
1. Eggs, cheese	Animal Pak
Oats, toast	
2. Tuna, salad, apple, avocado	BCAA
3 Fruit, nuts and dates	
4 Venison, salad, apple and rye bread	Animal Pak
	BCAA at bed

Foods seem to be better now, I was trying to eat too much. Weight has settled back to 145 or so I was 148 – 149 before Christmas.

Feel better at this weight.

Nut balls

You will have seen these here and there, very good for long days out hiking, or as a meal replacement.

Put in a bowl a big dollop of nut butter – two heaped table spoon or three. Mixed seeds – ground almonds, desiccated coconut. Table spoon or two each, more of the ground coconut.

If you like the flavour, handful of raisins – hand full of oats, big spoon of honey.

Mix together with a smidge of water and put in fridge for an hour.

Take out shape into balls and then put back in fridge until they firm up - no cooking, they are good to go.

They will also keep for days.

Monday 2 March 2020, 144¾

Squat free, 1 x 50

Band squats, 3 x 20

Sissy squat, 3 x 20

Walked five miles, 2 at night also with back pack on, 16 pound weight

Just messing about with training until something settles in at the moment. Been hiking then when I get in I've been doing odd workouts as if is the end of the day on the trail to get a feel for training on the trail. I have even mapped out a plan for the trail as far as what days we will train in a gym – at a town – and what we will do with bands on the other days.

Foods eaten

Foods	Supplements
	BCAA
1. Eggs x 3, oats, raisins, dates	Animal Pak
2. Tuna, avocado, apple, rye bread	
3. Nut ball and fruit	
4. Tuna, rice and salad	Animal Pak
5. Yogurt and granola	
	BCAA at bed

Little plan out

Start hike on the South West Coast Path – Sunday 14 March 2021, Mother's Day

1000 miles is the goal in 12 weeks. Twice a week staying in Bed & Breakfasts, the rest of the time camping, Jo and I.

Start on Sunday 14 March 2021.

Monday	Settle into hike and surroundings
Tuesday	All body weights workout at a town gym – big basics
Wednesday	Rest – just hike
Thursday	Chest and back band workout on trail
Friday	All body weights workout at town gym – big basics
Saturday	Rest – just hike
Sunday	Shoulders and arms band workout on trail
Monday	All body weights workout at a town gym – big basis
Tuesday	Rest – just hike
Wednesday	Legs band workout on trail
Thursday	All body weights workout in town gym – big basics
Friday	Rest – just hike
Saturday	Band work on trail chest and back
Sunday	All body weights workout at town gym – big basics
Monday	Rest – just hike

...and so on and so on.

Two all body workouts a week – two band workouts a week. Rotating, chest and back, shoulders and arms, legs, with bands over two weeks – two days doing something, one day off after main weight days. Will try to time workouts with weights at B&Bs in towns on trail.

Tuesday 3 March 2020

Workout – shape week shoulders and arms

Did this very fast

	Weight	Reps
Lat raise	30lb	20, 12, 12
Press machine	40kg, 50kg, 60kg	All 12
Rear lat raise	25lb	3 sets 12
Dumbbell curl	30lb	12, 12, 10
Pushdown	30kg	15, 15, 10
Barbell curl	75lb	8, 8, 6
Extensions (hammer curl bar)	? weight	12, 12, 10

Later four mile walk – no rucksack – legs sore from band workout yesterday – "odd but good". Just testing out all band workouts to see how we can use them on trail. The bands I have are very strong Lifeline USA TNT bands, the best I have used over the years.

Food	Supplements
	BCAA

1. Eggs, oats, fruit
2. Pro after training, BCAA, Glutamine and Creatine
3. Nut ball, yogurt and apple   Brewer's yeast and Vit C
4. Nuts and dates   Animal Pak
5. Rice, tuna and salad
6. Yogurt, raisins, berries

2685 (low but okay), try to hover around 3000 – that's better for me.

Food I ate while on holidays.

1. 3 eggs, oats, cheese
2. Pro and fruit
3. Bread, nut butter, yogurt and fruit
4. Same as 2
5. Tuna, or eggs, rice and veg
6. Yogurt and pro, berries and nut butter or oats pro nut butter

This was so easy to do on hols, foods were very easy to get and also in the hotel.

Wednesday 4 March 2020, 144¾

Helped Molly and Josh move so didn't eat as much.

1. Eggs, bread, oats, honey   Animal Pak BCAA and Vit C, BY
2. Nuts and fruit
3. Bread, nuts and fruit   Same supps
4. Rice veg and tuna
5. Yogurt and granola   Same supps

Spent the day out with the kids – great fun. With a huge white van I borrowed off my mate Vince.

Full day of working and moving stuff – house is lovely.

Took food with me.

Thursday 5 March 2020, 143¾ Busy yesterday lost weight

Legs – shape week

	Weight	Reps
Abs		20
Rope crunch		
Leg tucks side bends		3 x round
Side bends		
Calves standing	100kg	3 x 20
Seated	55kg	3 x 20
Leg extension	5 plates	15 – 15
Leg press	3 plates a side	15 – 15
Squats	80kg	15 – 15

Foods eaten

	Food	Supplements	Calories
1.	Eggs x 3	(Animal Pak, 2 BY, 1 Vit C)	270
	Small toast		150
	Honey		100
	Oats		180
	Cinnamon		
2.	Pro after training		250
3.	Bread		150
	Nut butter		100
	Apple		100
	Yogurt		220
4.	Nuts		200
	Dates		200
5.	Rice	(Animal Pak, 2 BY, 1 Vit C)	180
	Tuna		150
	Veg		50
	Oil		50
6.	Granola		460
	Yogurt		220
			3030

Friday 6 March 2020, 144.5

No walks – busy day as had Wednesday off.
Bit of yoga at night before bed.
Looking forward to training in the morning.

Foods eaten

	Food	Supplements	Calories
1.	Eggs	Animal Pak, 2 BY, 1 Vit C	270
	Bread		150
	Honey		100
	Oats with cinnamon		180
			700 total
2.	Nuts		250
	Fruit		180
3.	Bread (large)		250
	Nut butter		100
	Fruit		100
	Yogurt		220
4.	Nuts		180
	Fruit		140
5.	Chicken and cashew nuts with rice at Kings with Molly and Josh		850
			2970 - good

Saturday 6 March 2020, 145 – holding water from meal last night

Training – Chest and back

Bench press	60kg x 12, 65kg x 10, 70kg x 8
With pull downs	55 x 12, 60 x 10, 65 x 8
Incline dumbbell	40lb x 12, 45lb x 10, 50lb x 8
With low pulley row wide bar	45kg x 12, 50kg x 10, 55kg x 8
Flyes	40lb, 3 x 10
With shrugs -with half deadlifts to just below the knee	100kg, 3 x 10
Pull overs	45lb, 3 x 12
With sit up roman chair	3 x 20
And leg tucks	3 x 20

Foods eaten

	Food	Supplements	Calories
1.	Eggs	Animal Pak, Vit C, 2 BY	270
	Bread		100
	Butter		100
	Oats		180
			650 total
2.	BCAA after training with rice cakes		100
3.	Tuna and rice		250
4.	Fish		250
	Potatoes		250
	Bread		100
5.	Oats		360
	Pro		120
	Berries		140
			2220

Sunday 7 March 2020

No training
Walked for one hour, tired today was a hard week

Foods eaten

	Foods	Supplements
		BCAA first thing
1.	Eggs x 3, Oats, Raisins	Animal Pak, 2 Aminos before meal
2.	Chicken, rice, veg	2 Aminos before meal
		1 Vit C 2 BY
3.	Same as 2	2 Aminos beforehand
4.	Beef, 2 small homemade burgers, spuds and broccoli	
5.	Yogurt and pro mix, 1 spoon nut butter	2 Aminos beforehand
		Bedtime - BCAAs

Monday 8 March 2020, 144 ¾ look lean and full

Walked around 3 miles.
Very busy day with work.

Foods eaten

Foods	**Supplements**
1. Eggs, oats, raisins	Animal Pak, 2 Aminos before meal
2. Nuts and banana	
3. Bread, nut butter, yogurt and fruit	2 Aminos beforehand
4. Chicken and salad	2 Aminos beforehand
5. Yogurt, granola and pro	
	BCAAs at bedtime

Tuesday 10 March 2020, 145 BCAAs and Aminos filling me out a bit

Training

Shoulder and arms focus

	Weight	**Reps**
Lat raise seated	25lb	10, 10, 10
Press machine	2 plates	10
	3 plates	10, 10
Upright row	60lb	X 10
Push down	30kg	x 12, 3 rounds
Curls	70lb	10, 8, 8
Extensions Dumbbell	25lb	10
Dumbbell curl seated	30lb	8, 6, 3 rounds
Crossovers	25kg	15
Leg extensions	4 plates	15
Bent over rows	70lb	15, 3 rounds
Dumbbell squat	35lb each hand	15
Neck rear		3 x 15, 3 rounds
Wrist curls	60lb	3 x 10

Did all this in 40 minutes.

Did some yoga late on.

Foods eaten

Foods	Supplements
	BCAA first thing
1. 3 eggs 3 whites	Animal Pak, 2 Aminos, 1 Vit C, 2 BY
2 toast – olive oil butter	
2. Pro after training plus BCAA	
3. Rye bread, 2 eggs and an apple	
4. Nuts, raisins, seeds	
5. Quiche, rice, salad	2 Aminos, 2 BY, 1 Vit C
5. Yogurt and granola	
	BCAA at bed

Wednesday 11 March 2020, 144.5 – 10 weeks 3 days until powerlifting meet

Walked 5 miles

Yoga at night – all body – ready for tomorrow

Foods eaten

Foods	Supplements
1. Eggs x 2, Oats, raisins, banana, all scrambled up, with coconut oil	As normal
2. Bread, nut butter, cottage cheese, apple	
3. Nuts, seeds and raisins	
4. Quiche, rice and salad	
5. Oats, milk, bran, nut butter, raisins	

Thursday 12 March 2020, 145.5

Awesome session

Skips 200 – rower 50

Squats warm up then		80 x 5, 100 x 5, 110 x 5	
Leg extension	4 plates,	15, 15, 15	
Leg press	4 plates,	15, 15, 15	
Standing leg curl	3 plates	12, 10, 8	
Dips		15, 10, 10	
Chins		10, 8, 8	
Bent over lat	20lb	10, 10, 10	
All very slow and strict lots of tension in muscle			
Cable preacher curl	3 plates	15, 15, 15	
Rope pushdown	20kg	15, 15, 15	
Calf raise	110kg	3 x 15, different toes each 5 reps	

Real good session, also all done in 50 minutes.

Walked 5 miles later also.

Foods eaten

Doing experiments with food at the moment, trying one at moment like I did for my 50th birthday shoot.

Lean meats fruit and veg and fruit and nuts, as if I am hiking all day. Trying to set it up so I can follow it all the time while on trail.

Food	**Supplements**
1. Eggs x 3, toast and honey	Animal Pak, BCAA, Aminos, Vit C and BY
2. Pro, BCAAS after training	
3. Chicken and salad, pear	
4. Tuna, avocado, salad and apple	
5. Yogurt, berries, 2 scoop oats	

Thursday notes

More water!!

Was up at 03:50, quick bath and walk with the Doo (Daisy Doo our Spaniel) had a couple of clients early on, so only short walk with her.

Workout was awesome – loads of focus and feeling and moved very fast, all done in 50 minutes - including warm ups.

Skipping and rower seemed to bring my heart up quicker and warm my legs up better. All the moves today I did slow and with loads of control, but moved fast – as in not much rest if any, between them.

Food I did as if out all day – in fact I have worked outside all day and even ate my meals outside.

Hiked later on with 12lb pack on for 5 miles. Stopped for a coffee overlooking Emley Moore. Walked very fast and did as many hills as I could.

Yoga at night before bed.

Friday 13 March 2020

No training today

Walked 2 miles as to recover for big hike tomorrow, Bridlington cliff top one to do 'fast'.

Fair busy day but finished early.

Foods eaten

Food	Supplements
Green tea and honey	BCAA first thing
1. Oats, eggs, banana and honey	Animal Pak, Aminos, 2 BY, 2 Vit C
2. Cottage cheese, nuts and seeds	
3. Nuts, dates, pineapple and mango dried, tea and honey	
4. Tuna, salad, spud and avocado	
5. Greek yogurt	Animal Pak, Aminos, 2 BY, 2 Vit C
	BCAA before bed

Friday notes and prep for tomorrow

Needed a rest up today, legs kill from yesterday - it was a hard and fast workout and fast hike in afternoon.

Prepped all food for tomorrow's hike, 14 – 15 miles with lots of steps and hills, and weight in pack not much, but some.

Foods set out already for morning – fruit, apples, pears, banana, in bags – nuts, almonds and walnuts.

Dried fruit – pineapple and mango (no sulphates no sugar).

Blueberries organic – not dried.

Also made some nut balls.

In a tub, I mixed up nut butter, desiccated coconut, ground almond, pumpkin and sunflower seeds, organic honey, and a small amount of oats.

Just plopped enough for two in a bowl, these were golf ball sized balls. I mixed it up and refrigerated it for an hour to set. Job done. All you have to do is form them into balls and they will set. If they are too dry add a smidge of water.

Saturday 14 March 2020, 144 – look very lean an full

Up at 04:20

No training today going to do tomorrow

Plan was to hike today, so we set off early for Bridlington.

Foods eaten

Foods	Supplements
1. Eggs x 3, cheese, toast and honey	
2. Nut balls	Aminos
3. Trail mix, I made – in it was nuts, almonds and walnuts, pineapple and mango dried, blueberries, and a few raisins	Aminos
4. Small fish, no chips	Aminos
5. After walk and back at cabin	
Goats cheese, beans and rice, camping pack vegetable – rye bread	
6. Organic chocolate (cheat)	
	BCAA at bed

Notes

Goats cheese was raw and blue, bought at Field & Fawcett shop on our way to Bridlington. Bloody best cheese I have ever tasted.

14 miles done fast over cliff tops, I did 2 miles first thing also. We practically ran the steps, some 600 or so all told there and back. Foods were good as always, plus I took in some Aminos with meals and also in-between meals.

Awesome fresh air.

Sunday 15 March 2020

Training at home after we got back from cabin, at 14:30 – with Jo and Debs.

Chest, bench heavy first to a top 5 of 80kg

Incline fly	17.5kg	15, 15, 15
Chins		15, 15, 15
Dips (no weight)		15, 12, 10
Bent over row	50kg	15, 10, 10
Cable band curl		3 x 12
Lat raise	7kg	3 x 12
Pushdowns (chest expander)		3 x 10 each arm

No legs as sore from Thursday and all hiking I have done over last few days. Walked two miles prior to training as warm up. Yoga at bedtime also, leg type recovery - yoga.

Foods eaten

Food	Supplements
1. Eggs and cheese, rye bread with honey	Animal Pak, 2BY, 1 Vit C, 2 Aminos
2. Half a nut ball, banana	Aminos
3. Cottage cheese, nuts, raisins, pear	2 BY, 1 Vit C
4. Banana, BCAA after training – Tea and honey	
5. Tuna, veg, spud with olive oil	
6. Muesli, dried fruit, yogurt	2BY, 1 Vit C, 2 Aminos
7. Goats milk warm at bed, BCAA	

Notes – on way back from Cabin normally see hawks and deer, not this time. We did see about 150 geese though flying in formation.

Monday 16 March 2020, 144.5 look lean and full

Had a lay in today 05:30.

2 miles first thing, no weight added.

4 miles afternoon.

2 miles later on, with weight 16lb pack.

Foods eaten

Food	Supplements
	BCAA first thing
1. 4 eggs, cheese, seeded bread and honey	Animal Pak, 2BY, 1 Vit C, 2 Aminos
2. Cottage cheese, nuts - almonds and walnuts, seeds mixed. Pineapple and mango dried	2BY, 1 Vit C, 2 Aminos
3. Nuts and dates	
4. Tuna, spud and veg, olive oil	2BY, 1 Vit C, 2 Aminos
5. Muesli and yogurt	
	BCAA at bed

Notes of interest

My diet is as healthy as I can make it, after years of study this type of eating plan suits my lifestyle and goals. The goal is to hike The South Coast Path next year from around this date now, but do 1000 miles over a 12 week period.

The foods I eat are as if I am on the trail already – healthy quick foods, easy to get, and easy to prep and eat on the move. I take some supplements, and will give a rundown of each and why.

Let's cover the first – AP, you will note in my daily diary of foods and supplements.

This is Animal Pak vitamins and minerals – these packs have been around for many years and whenever I have been really lean I have taken them as a safeguard to health and to make sure I am not missing out on anything nutrient wise.

I was once so lean prepping for a show that I was dragging my feet and felt incredibly fatigued.

I got some Animal Pak vitamins and that same day taking them I felt like I had been given a new lease of life, the energy I had was like night and day. I was obviously lacking something, or many things. So since that day when I am low in weight like now, I take them.

Tuesday 17 March 2020, 144¾

Training

Warm up – 300 skips and 100 rower

Sit ups		3 x 20
Leg raise		3 x 20

Deadlifts in rack, pin 2 holes		Up to a top 5 of 3.5 plates a side, 160kg
Lat raise	30lb	12, 10, 8
Press machine	2.5 plates	12, 12, 12
Upright row	55lb	12, 10, 8
Cross overs	25kg	20, 15, 15
Pulldown	50kg	15, 15, 15
Pushdown rope	20kg	15, 15, 15
Curl	60lb	12, 12, 12
Leg extension	4 plates	20, 20, 20
But lifted with both legs lowered with right leg – weak right leg		
Walking lunges	No weight	40, 40, 40

Walked 1 mile lunchtime, 3 miles at night, pack on 16lb, lots of hills and climbs

Foods eaten

Food	Supplements
	BCAA first thing
1. 4 eggs, cheese, and toast with honey	AP, 2BY, 1 Vit C, 2 Aminos
2. Pro, Banana and BCAA after training	
3. Nando's with kids, sweet potato pitta	
4. Nuts, almonds, walnuts and raisins, dried pineapple and mango, seeds	2BY, 1 Vit C, 2 Aminos
5. Cheese, rye bread, tea and honey, apple	2BY, 1 Vit C, 2 Aminos
6. Apple, dates, small amount of granola, and yogurt	
Yoga at bed	BCAA

Notes of interest

Awesome books on nutrition.

Nutrition is an area I have read about and studied all of my life.

I am and always have been fascinated by the subject. Two books that have really resonated with me are...

Nutrition and Physical Degeneration by Weston A Price

Written in the 1920s Weston travelled the world observing how each race ate and lived, documenting everything regarding the foods they ate and how healthy or not they were.

This I found very interesting as how your great great grandparents ate and where they originated from is very important, how they ate even more so. Not just them but also before them, as you will find, as he did, that if they ate foods from their natural habitat they were devoid of illness. In short, if you ate foods that suited your own genetic makeup you won't go far wrong in all areas of health.

For instance I have Latvian and Scottish in my heritage, and funny as it sounds I eat like my grandad, and his dad before him and my great grandfather. Thick rye bread, milk and milk products, eggs, fish, oats, and lots of veg and salads. The more I have these foods as a base the better I look, feel, and perform.

Are you confused by Paavo Airola

An awesome book that covers much of the above in Weston's book but in more detail as to my ancestry – covering many foods eaten in Russia and Latvia, and many other healthy strong races. This book also covers many good recipes, and what foods do what for your system, and also covers what you may need.

A very old book but very good.

Anything by Bill Pearl

My mentor and hero in bodybuilding – it was Bill who recommended the above book by Paavo.

Wednesday 18 March 2020, 145

Up 03:00 put on slow cooker then back to bed for a couple of hours.

In slow cooker – sweet potato, cabbage, swede, carrots, onions, two foil packed tuna, in olive oil no drain ones. Tin of organic lentil and potato soup. This is a meal I may cook up on trail on our free days. Off day from hiking, just in a pan.

This cooked all day from 03:00 to around 17:00 in the slow cooker, it was lovely.

Foods eaten

Food	Supplements
	BCAA at 03:00
1. Oats, raisins, banana, nuts, goats milk	AP, 2BY, 1 Vit C, 2 Aminos
2. Rye bread, peanut butter, yogurt	2BY, 1 Vit C, 2 Aminos
3. Bit of organic chocolate	
4. Tuna stew as above, had this with thick black rye bread	2BY, 1 Vit C, 2 Aminos
5. Yogurt and muesli	
	BCAA before bed

Notes on supplements

BCAAs and Aminos

You may note in my notes that I take BCAA and Aminos. Now Aminos are just normal full spectrum amino acids that I have been taking with meals to add to the protein quality I am eating, making the food I eat even better. I have also been taking these on long walks so that my body does not tap into lean tissue for energy, or the amino acids needed whilst I am hiking hard. I am very lean at the moment and not much body fat is there for energy for the body under long duration work.

I chopped and changed my supplements around and towards end of last year, and early this year I made great use of liver tablets. These are again a great protein energy source and also high in iron, vitamin B and minerals. It's not that I am huge on eating lots of protein, but I want the best quality to be absorbed by my body.

BCAA are the most effective types of amino acids you can take when training hard and under stress. They comprise of three essential amino acids that are used by the body under extreme stress i.e. hard training and other stressors. They are Leucine, Isoleucine, and Valine.

Training is a stress and hiking miles is also a type of stress. BCAA are highly anabolic in a natural way and lower oestrogen levels in male and females. If you lower those levels – the anabolic balance can tip in your favour. This will – without a doubt make you leaner and more muscular.

Note I take them morning and night and also around workouts. These are the times I think they are best utilised by the body.

One of the best supplements and best anti-ageing supplements a body builder and fitness enthusiast can take.

I will rotate again soon, and again use liver and some other supplements I think I need at the time and what I think my body needs.

BY is Brewer's Yeast – high in B complex, for energy.

Vit C is for recovery and immune system.

Thursday 19 March 2020, 145

Training

100 row warm ups.

Only did squats for legs as they still ached from other day.

Squats - no weight then warmed up	80kg x 5, 100kg x 5, 110 x 5, 120 x 5
Dumbbell chest press	30lb, 20, 40 x 15, 45 x 12
Low rows	50kg x 20, 60 x 15, 65 x 12
Lat raise	15lb, 20, 20lb x 15, 20 x 12
Pushdown V Bar	30kg, 15, 15, 15
Dumbbell curls	30lb, 12, 12 12
Calf - change toe positions each set	100kg, 15, 15, 15

Walked 2 miles in morning and 2 miles in afternoon. Steady as needed to recover.

Foods eaten

Food	**Supplements**
	BCAA first thing
1. Oat scramble*	AP, 2BY, 1 Vit C, 2 Aminos
2. Cliff bar and protein after training	BCAA
3. Cottage cheese, mixed up with nuts and raisins, and some dried pineapple	
4. Few nuts and dates, apple	2BY, 1 Vit C, 2 Aminos
5. Tuna, stew I made yesterday with soda bread	
6. Muesli and yogurt	
	BCAA at bed

*Oat Scramble Recipe

4 eggs

8oz oats

2 bananas chopped

Handful raisins

Scramble in a pan with coconut oil until golden brown

Serves two – add honey when cooked

Notes on training at present

I always know when training is going well because I am ravenous – I cannot eat enough –and I have a very good appetite.

Training at the moment as you can see has no set-in-stone pattern to it and that is done for a reason.

The tail end of last year and early this I have followed a basic one set per exercise to fail, training quite heavy for this point in my life. It worked very well and I got stronger and fuller and felt good. But then it took its toll as it does if you keep pushing, over-training was creeping up, at that point I took to a lighter but much more freestyle training program.

Freestyle is derived from Dave Draper an ex-Mr Universe that said after years of regimented programs he got to the point where he enjoyed his training more when the restraints had been removed.

Every now and then I feel like this and prefer to let my body tell me what I need, I have trained long enough now to be able to eb and flow, ride the wave in the workout so to speak.

This I feel gives me some incredible workouts and results.

The goal is at present is to move fast and be so fit and healthy for the 1000 mile hike next year so I am training to not only be strong, fit and fast but also agile.

You will note that on each session I give priority to a big base move then just knock the shit out of the rest of the workout – go by how I feel, what works and what doesn't, what I did before. So on and so on. So there is a slight method to the madness, basically I listen to my body.

Today for instance, we would normally do more legs but they were very sore from the other day so I just squatted.

I also prefer at this stage in my training life to train all body each session, with any part either getting a lot of work or just a flush of a few sets of work.

Friday 20 March 2020, 145

First thing this morning two mile walk with no weight.

Mid-afternoon after a bit of working with clients, then walked five miles, added only small pack 6lb but did lots of hills.

Stopped for a coffee I had with me and watched a Kestrel hunting. It's a place I normally stop and I know their nest is near. It hovered in the air on the wind – and today was very windy – it seemed effortless to it.

On a side note up at the cabin on one of our walks when over at the coast, there was two what I thought to be Kestrels nesting. These were a little chunkier then other Kestrels. Having got home I looked in my book on birds and I think they are Merlins, look very similar to Kestrels, but thicker-set. It is also on marshland where Merlins like to nest. Later in the day at home saw a Black Kite, hunting some small birds at the back of my house – awesome day of seeing some amazing bird life.

Foods eaten

Food	Supplements
Strong coffee	BCAA first thing

1. Oats, pro, nuts, raisins, milk

   This can be bagged up and taken anywhere eaten hot or cold or with milk as this morning cold. If camping I can just boil up water or milk and add to it and stir and eat.

2. Rye bread toast, honey and banana	2 Amino, 1 Vit C, 2 BY
3. Eggs x 4, cheese, sourdough bread	2 Amino, 1 Vit C, 2 BY
4. Nuts and dates, dried pineapple and few raisins, tea and honey	
5. Tuna and rice, veg	2 Amino, 1 Vit C, 2 BY
6. Muesli and yogurt	

Yoga before bed

Saturday 21 March 2020

No cabin this week, trained at home as all gyms are closed due to virus. Chilled at Cho's (Jo's nickname) then only had a small walk, Daisy very tired after a week of hard walks with me, bless her.

Workout – very good

Fly	20, 15, 12
Pull downs	20, 15, 12
Bench press	20, 15, 10
Bent over row	20, 15, 15
Lat raise	12, 12, 12
Curl	12, 12, 12
Bench dip	15, 15, 15
Leg extension	20, 20, 20
French squat	20, 20, 20

French squat – named after Serge Nubret who performed these in his leg workouts, it's a bottom position free hand squat where you go right down and only half way back up keeping tension on quads. Feet – heels are on two small weight plates to make you stress the front quads also.

I've done these for years on and off - I started doing them at 14.

Foods eaten

Foods	Supplements
Strong coffee	BCAA first thing
1. Oat scramble as described before	AP, 1 Vit C, 2 BY
2. Trained then BCAA and fruit	
3. Cheese sarnie, with soda bread organic cheese and an apple	2 Aminos, 1 Vit C, 2 BY
4. Goats cheese and onion tart, spuds and veg	2 Aminos, 1 Vit C, 2 BY
5. Granola and yogurt	
6. Organic chocolate, goats milk	
	BCAA before bed

Notes on food

I try to get all organic food where I can, I also try to get everything wholegrain – whole wheat – full fat, there are no preservatives at all in anything that I get.

You may also note that I very rarely eat any chicken, beef, or turkey, this is because I find it hard to digest these days, so I very rarely eat it as noted.

I found milk products, cheese, goats milk and eggs provide a better digestible protein for myself.

Years ago I would limit these for fear of "smoothing out", and them not being as clean a fuel source, but in fact they provide prefect fuel and protein and many other benefits for me. I feel awesome on the foods I eat, can train hard, walk forever, recover well and to be honest I am as sharp as my competing days. Even with the ton of carbs I eat.

All the activity I do allows for the volume of food.

Move more and eat more guys.

You may also note I was counting calories earlier in my journals, this was because I was trying to gain some weight and go up to 150lb or so, or slightly more, but I soon decided I felt better being 5 – 7lb lighter. So I just eat and let my body settle and this is its natural set point so it seems. I can eat a huge amount as you can see and stay the same weight. If I drop a bit too much I just eat up. If I feel like I am not as light and fast I will ease up a bit. Simple.

If I have a cheat meal other than the foods on my list its only now and then, like a fish from the chip shop over at the coast or a bar of organic chocolate. I only cheat though when I feel I have earned it. Like extra hard training or a really long fast hike, then I feel the need for a calorie boost.

Sunday 22 March 2020, 145¼

Walked only a mile with the Doo, as she was limping with her left leg – she has a bit of arthritis in it and it flares up now and then. Rest and some olive oil on her meals makes her like a pup again in a few days.

So I did 5 miles on my own – small back pack on - 6lb.

There are two woodland areas I go through and often hear a woodpecker at this time of year. But try as I might I cannot find him, will keep looking.

Stopped and had a coffee and nuts and dried fruit, took in the nature of this beautiful day.

Foods eaten

	Food	Supplements
1.	3 boiled eggs, 3 rye bread and honey, green tea and honey	AP, 2 Aminos, 1 Vit C, 2 BY
2.	Dried fruit, dates pineapple, raisins, almonds	
3.	Rice, half of the quiche, veg	2 Aminos
4.	Tuna, rice, veg	2 Aminos
5.	Granola, yogurt	2 Aminos
6.	Goats milk at bed	
	Yoga at bed	
		BCAAs before bed

Notes on nutrition

Years ago I once read an article by Bill Reynolds, a brilliant bodybuilder writer back in the 80s – 90s. It was the early 80s and I read an article by him on dried fruits and all their benefits, ever since I have always eaten them, and lots of them.

They are a store house of natural sugars vitamins and minerals and can be taken anywhere and kept for a long time also very light for hiking trails.

There was once a period of 9 years where I ate almonds and dates mixed together as a mid-afternoon meal/snack every day.

Mixed together these two make a perfect amino acid balanced meal of carbs, fats, proteins and a ton of vitamins and minerals.

I never forgot a line in his book or article, which said - fruits and dried fruits are the store of the suns natural energy.

Think about it – how good will they be for you.

I always make sure I get organic and sulphate free, fruit and dried fruit.

Honey, another staple of my eating plans and always has been. Honey is an antiseptic, antibiotic and is one of the best foods known to man. There is very rare a day where I do not have multiple spoons of honey. Many think of honey as a simple sugar it is actually a medium absorbed carb. Very, very good for you, again organic is a must.

Monday 23 March 2020, 144.5

Only 3 miles walked today. Had a busy day at home sorting out lots of stuff that needed doing in light of all the changes regarding the virus.

Did some yoga mid-afternoon – plenty of stretching and standing poses for balance and to loosen legs up.

Foods eaten

Foods	Supplements
	BCAAS first thing
1. Oat scramble	AP, 2 Aminos, 1 Vit C, 2 BY
2. Nuts, pineapple and raisins	
3. Rye bread, peanut butter, apple, yogurt	2 BCAA
4. Tuna, veg, spud and oil	2 Aminos
5. Muesli and yogurt	2 Aminos
	BCAAs at bed

Notes on training

Over the years I have spent time getting stronger and with that comes size. I have found as I have aged I cannot train as heavy as I used to, and to be honest you shouldn't it's far too risky. You are much more susceptible to injury and that would put a halt to training completely.

So I move quicker between sets increasing the intensity. I don't do the reps fast I may add – everything I do is very controlled and with upmost concentration involved. This way the muscle is worked as hard as it can be but within a safe zone.

I also move fast as to increase the cardio effect of training so the heart is elevated and worked as hard as my muscles. I want to be fit and healthy into older age and plodding about lifting heavy weights will not do that at all.

The hiking I do is also done at a very fast pace in order to increase fitness and cardio vascular efficiency.

I often hike with a rucksack on with added weight which makes the body work much harder.

Another string to my bow is yoga, I do this most nights whilst watching TV or before a bath – nothing fancy just some basic moves that make me feel loose and good.

Tuesday 24 March 2020, 144½

Workout home – total lock down of country – all I am seeing is my kids and Jo.

Louis is off work so I am getting to see him a lot and with me not working also see Jo more. So out of the bad there is some good. I suspect more families will be feeling this also.

We are allowed to go to shops, which me and Jo do, and one walk – so I went out and did 5 miles, with not a soul near me.

Training

300 lunges in the field back of my house

*Up the rack lat raise and down	5, 6, 7, 8, 8, 9, 10, 12.5kg – all sets of 12 and then back down to 9kg
⌐ Cross overs	15, 15, 15
Rows TNT band	15, 15, 15
Extensions dumbbell	15, 15, 15
∟ Curls bar	12, 12, 12

That was it. Then the walk mentioned 5 miles no weight added.

Foods eaten

Food	Supplements
	BCAA first thing
1. Muesli and granola, goats milk	2 Aminos
2. Pro after training, rice cakes	
3. Cheese, rye bread and an apple	2 Aminos
4. Apple and banana, nuts tea and honey	2 Aminos
5. Tuna, rice and veg, stir fried veg in olive oil added cooked rice when done and tuna	2 Aminos
6. Granola and Greek yogurt	BCAA at bed

Run out of other supplements. Will get some more when all this is over. Foods more important now than spending on supplements.

*Up and down the rack – is very good – here is what I did. It works well on many moves, not just lat raises.

I grabbed the 6kg dumbbells did 12, walked and put them back on the rack, took off 7kg, did 12, walked back got 8kgs did 12 and so on and so on, until I had enough and it felt hard to get 12. Then I came down a few sets of dumbbells in the same way. Huge pump in the shoulders. You may note that I group moves together like this "[". This just puts three or more moves together non-stop and the reps are listed on the 3 rounds a I call them.

Like I said before I am moving very fast and attacking each session to elevate the heart rate also as well as work my body hard.

Wednesday 25 March 2020, 144 ½

Walked two miles 6lb pack.

Later a run in the fields out back of our house two miles, then 150 lunges to cool off.

Very hot day. 16 or so degrees for this time of year very good.

I thought I would run as cannot do the miles I would normally do as I am staying close to home. The fields behind my house are just over the back fence for me and I can run and lunge round there and not see anybody. This got my heart rate up and I felt awesome after. Will do more until lock down lifts.

Foods eaten

	Food	Supplements
	Green tea and honey first thing	BCAA
1.	Oats, bran, raisins, apple, goats milk, nuts and cinnamon – read notes for prep of this	2 Aminos
2.	Fruit and nuts	2 Aminos
3.	Rye bread, nut butter, yogurt and apple	
4.	Fruit and nuts	2 Aminos
5.	Tuna, casserole, cooked in slow cooker from early this morning, had rye bread with it.	
	I have mentioned this before in my recipes.	

Notes on day and nutrition

Breakfast

The night before breakfast here is a good way of prepping an awesome tasting breakfast.

I use a protein scoop – out of my tub, I am guessing is about an ounce of each of these. In a bowl I do four scoops oats, one scoop, bran, one scoop raisins, one scoop almonds. I then grate an apple into all of this with a cheese grater and then add cinnamon, and cover it all with goats milk and mix. I put it into the fridge and now leave overnight. In the morning add a splash of goats milk so it's not so thick or a dollop of yogurt.

This is awesome as the apple seeps into the milk the raisins plump up and the nuts soften. with the cinnamon added it is very, very good.

Water

I drink 2 litres of Evian a day, along with some green teas and honey for my hydration.

The diet I am on is also very good for hydration and for not "drying" you out like an old prune like all these low carb diets do.

The foods I eat are high in water content – veg, fruit, and the like, as your body draws fluid from them also.

Supplements

I have run out of supplements at the moment, but will in the next week or so restock on them. My thoughts are on going back to liver and brewer's yeast again over the next stage of training.

Thursday 26 March 2020, 144½

Training at home – no gyms – but I have an excellent home gym set up. Jo and I did only legs today to give them a good shock. Weather was beautiful so we squatted outside.

Exercise	Weight	Reps
Leg extensions	30kg	25 – 20
Leg press – machine squat (2 rounds of these)	50kg	25 – 20
Squat	50kg	25 20
Leg curls		15 15 15
Stiff leg deadlifts		15 15 15
Calves (later on in the day)		
Standing		3 x 25
Crunches		3 x 20
Leg tucks		3 x 20

Foods eaten

	Food	Supplements
		BCAA first thing
1.	Oat scramble	2 Aminos
2.	Protein, rice cakes	BCAA
3.	Tuna, cottage cheese, mixed together, boiled potatoes and peas	2 Aminos
4.	Cup of tea and honey, BCAA after calves and abs session	
5.	Turkey, rice and veg	2 Aminos

Very rare I have meat, but was cooking it for Louis and thought what the heck. I cannot eat it for more than a few days without it – for want of a better word – 'bunging' me up

6. Oats, milk, protein, egg whites, raisins, water or milk or both, cooked in a big pan, again Louis and I. This makes the oats really creamy and very nice.

Outside

After years of competing – my life and business being wrapped up in it, I found it hard to adjust to a more normal life, if you will. Think about this, I had been competing since I was 15 years old, and my last competition I think I was 45/46 or so. I would have still been doing it I guess if it was not for a serious injury on my leg.

Every year – prepping for a qualifier, the British and Worlds. Year upon year. This along with my business helping others do the same completely consumed me.

It wasn't until my late wife Louise fell ill and consequently passed away that I realised I had worked far too much and been far too selfish.

At first, I turned myself in-ward, angry at myself and life, I could not figure everything out and it tore at me every minute.

Then I turned that pain and anger into a positive energy - outwardly helping others and raising money for charity.

Not wanting to sound a dick here, but I also had to find myself again. This was where my kids and my now partner Jo came in, I now felt alive again and had purpose. But that said I was still lost without goals and direction.

Then I remembered what I was like when I was a kid – how I was out all the time. I was nature mad, before the iron bug took a hold of me.

So, I started hiking, camping, just being as much as I could around and in nature. All the excitement and wonder of nature that was with me as a kid, came flooding back into my life and nature – tended to heal me.

This also gave me the obsession I needed. I need an obsession, a healthy one and this fit the bill. I found myself studying nature, camping, miles walked, sleeping bags, tents, fires, meals cooked while outside, birds, wildlife, trails and countless other things. I now had a new goal and direction that I could do until the end of my days. Luckily, Jo feels the same and loves being out with me sharing all we see, and we do see some wonders that will take your breath away.

This outdoor life turned into "how can we make this an adventure", having read adventure books all my life and being stuck in the four walls of a gym for most of it, I wanted to experience and feel adventure, something big.

At first we/I settled on doing the Appalachian Trail in the USA – for the early start of 2021. An adventure that would take 6 months of hiking and cover 2180 miles.

After I sat down and tackled the logistics of this, it soon became apparent that I could not afford it as my daughter Molly is due to get married this year to a wonderful guy, Josh.

Molly has to come first and my kids always will.

So what now? Well that turned into a blessing in disguise as after having read The Salt Path by Raynor Winn I soon realised there was an amazing trail right here in this country – The South Coast West Path. From Minehead all the way around the coast, and ending up at Poole in Dorset some 630 miles, as this awesome book depicts.

This I structured and costed right down to the last quid the best I could. We now had a new goal that was far more affordable, the Appalachian trail can be done another time.

So we are planning on doing the trail in March of 2021 for 12 weeks. In 12 weeks covering 1000 miles on that trail to raise money for Marie Curie. A charity very close to my heart and many others.

Hence you will see throughout the book hikes and food ideas and so on as the goal is in sight. If you feel lost, down, and/or directionless, I urge you to give mother nature a try – her healing and inspirational powers – work wonders on your mind, soul and health.

Friday 27 March 2020, 144.5

Legs sore today, plenty of yoga later I think.

Being at home getting on top of all jobs, painting, cleaning, washing, writing and drawing.

Had a long day but good day – writing – and sorting house out. Rested today other than a big yoga session, as I have a huge workout planned tomorrow, plus some big walks/hiking.

Foods eaten

Food

1. Eggs x 3, cheese, big thick slices of rye bread toasted with honey

2. Pro, milk, nut butter

3. Rye bread, nut butter, yogurt, apple, a very good balanced quick meal and I have this often for lunch

4. Tuna and cottage cheese mixed, apple

5. Turkey (again making it for Louis) small serving lots of brown rice and veg, olive oil

6. Yogurt, nuts, and fruit

"Flex – don't just do – flex and feel"

I say this to clients all the time and every time I train I say it to myself - not out loud but in my mind "don't just do the reps feel them".

Moving a weight from A to B is not the be all and end all to a rep, and if you get the reps you were aiming for that does not automatically mean you are going to gain some muscle from that set.

Far from it – if you cannot feel this muscle, burning, searing pain and contraction – rep after rep – you will not grow.

If you are just throwing weights around all you are doing is a job, a manual labour job.

Every movement has to be worked with precision and focus, feel the stretch in the muscle, feel it, engage in the rep – feel it move the weight, not momentum, move the weight. But feel the muscle you are wanting to work, move the weight then at the top of the movement flex – yes flex and squeeze the muscle. Hold that squeeze then return the direction under control and again feel the negative, feel – feel.

It's the only way you will grow.

Yes weight is important you must get stronger to get bigger, but the muscle has to move the weight.

Another thing, the more burn and pain you can put up with, the more muscle fibres are being recruited and the more you will grow.

On a dumbbell chest press for instance I get an intense pain and contraction in my chest. I really have to fight and endure it. But the more I do, the next day the more I ache.

I know over the years, many have said that's not an indicator of growth – but I beg to differ – since I was 15 I have always aimed for an ache – if I didn't ache something was not right.

It always stood me in good stead then and now. Now you won't get an ache by throwing weights around, you have to move them and feel them.

Saturday 28 March 2020

First thing walked two miles – early on, just BCAAs, and tea and honey. Then I had breakfast before training.

Later 1 mile, then later still 3 miles, 6 in total.

Training

Bench press up to a top 5 – only got 85kg x 3

Dips	15
Chins	15 – 3 times round
Pulldowns	12
Rows machine	12 – 3 times round
Flyes	12
Curls	12
Pushdowns	15 – 3 times round

Foods eaten

	Food	**Supplements**
		BCAA first thing
1.	Oats 2 scoops, 2 scoop muesli, granola 2 scoops, 1 scoop pro, goats milk, small handful raisins	
	Huge breakfast calorie wise over 800 calories would need a good lot of calories today. It tasted awesome too.	
2.	Rye and Cranberry bread, nut butter, apple and a yogurt	2 Aminos
3.	After training protein and BCAA	
4.	Almonds, pineapple and dates, raisins	2 Aminos
5.	Pro	
6.	Tuna, rice and big salad, olive oil, bit of organic chocolate for afters	
7.	Granola and Greek yogurt	2 Aminos
		BCAA at bed

Notes on training

Bench press was done in the rack starting at the bottom on the pins, it is very hard but also a safe way of benching. As it takes all the momentum out of the movement.

Dips were done on my V bar dipping bars, knees tucked forward body in a half moon shape leaning into the movement. Elbows go out to the sides, not over stretching but elbows going to just a smidge below 90 degrees.

Tensing at the top – under no circumstances do your legs swing back behind you, they are always forward. This stresses the pecs massively.

Chins wide grip all the same all the way up (all the way down full range).

Pullovers - I do these laid across a bench, head slightly hanging over the bench edge. Hips off the other side of the bench – remember this is across the bench not lengthways. Now the hips must dip a little and be slightly lower than the upper body, shoulders stuck to the bench dumbbell is held on the inside plates both open palms gripping across the bottom plate. Bend the elbows slightly and have your arms not splayed out wide but sort of neutral and comfortable. Stretch back and over your head moving the dumbbell towards the floor feeling the stretch in your lats. It is important to keep your elbows locked in that slightly bent position and to not move them at all it's the upper arm that pivots back and down.

Pull the dumbbell using the strength of your lats to only eye level with your head hanging over the bench a little - any higher will take gravity off the dumbbell and off your lats, tension, tension, all the way. Stretch and squeeze.

Pullovers are an awesome lat exercise – without the aid of your biceps – combined with a row it is pure torture, the good kind.

Pullovers also work the pecs very well – the lower pec line at points in the movement and the upper pec right up near the clavicles in other areas of the movement. Awesome movement done right.

The workout was a fast focused one. Jo, Lou (Louis) and I. Lou stronger than me on bench, but got him on chins and dips ha-ha. Jo is strong all round.

I just wanted to note some moves to give you some tips, will do again on others.

Photo by Russell Clark

Sunday 29 March 2020, 144.5

Got a 5 mile walk in this morning, incorporated in these five miles I did 5 hill runs, a very steep hill near my home right after I did 300 lunges up a slight incline. By then my legs were shot. Trying to get other things in at moment to keep my fitness improving for the hike next year. At the moment we cannot go to the cabin or long hikes on a weekend because of the lockdown.

This is working very well though for the present time.

Try the lunges for overall fitness – cardio – and obviously leg work I also did 300 a day for 90 days straight a few years back in order to heal my leg injury and increase mobility back to normal – it works wonders and I got leaner also.

I do 300 now and then these days, and will over the next few weeks thrown them in more. After the walk run and lunges I had lots of water and BCAA. Later in the day I did another two miles and yoga, while watching TV in the evening. Good day loved it.

Foods eaten

	Food	Supplements
		BCAA first thing
1.	3 eggs and cheese, rye bread honey, oats, cinnamon`	2 Aminos
2.	Pro, goats milk, fruit	
3.	Small amount of beef I made for Lou, rice. I made a sauce for it, tomatoes, garlic, olive oil, tomato puree all blended up	
4.	Tuna, salad, apple, olive oil, cottage cheese	
5.	Yogurt, granola, dried fruit	2 liver, 2 BY, 1 vit C

Today I finished the last of my Aminos, I ran out of what I was using over a week ago. All I have left is a few BCAA and a bit of protein (whey). I don't use much whey lately as I like to eat rather than use lots of drinks. I use them when I am in a prep for something.

I waited to order some new supplements because I wanted to see if deliveries were still being done, for example Amazon and such. They are still working so I ordered the supplements that I was using just before Christmas on the photo shoots. Like I have said before I like to alternate what I use my favourites being over time – BCAA, Aminos, Whey, liver tablets, brewer's yeast, vitamin C and Animal Pak vitamins and minerals.

I am waiting today for a delivery of liver tablets, I use Universal ones, they are grass-fed and hormone free. Brilliant old school supplement, protein, Aminos, vitamins, minerals and iron. Awesome for energy, pump and recovery.

I take a shit load of these.

Here are some notes on other supplements I use.

Brewer's yeast

A storehouse of B vitamins, B vitamins have so many roles in your body and I think they are invaluable to the hard working bodybuilder/trainer, I use Solgar ones with added B12. Very good company.

Vitamin C

I use ones with Bioflavonoids in them as your body absorbs the vitamin C better. Awesome for recovery from hard workouts, a brilliant antioxidant and it is also good for hardness of the muscle as it builds the cement like structure in the muscle fibres, again Solgar.

My top four for a while.

Liver, Brewer's Yeast, Vitamin C and BCAA after training you will see them used with meals, as soon as I get them.

Monday 30 March 2020, 145¼

Had a good day writing and setting out this book you are holding.

Later I ran in the fields for 2¼ miles and did 300 lunges, 3 x 30 crunches and 3 x 30 leg raise all in the field.

Loved it – it was cold and windy but invigorating.

Trained Lou later he did legs.

Foods eaten

Food	Supplements
	BCAA first thing
1. Oats 4 scoops, 1 scoop bran, 5 dates chopped, apple finely chopped, small handful of raisins, cinnamon, goats milk. Cover and put in fridge overnight – by the morning the ingredients have soaked up the milk – add a touch more milk and enjoy. Tastes awesome.	2 liver 2 BY 1 vit C
2. Nuts, dates, raisins	2 liver 2 BY 1 vit C
3. Tuna, rice, veg, olive oil	2 liver 2 BY 1 vit C
4. BCAA after run and lunges	
5. Cottage cheese, nuts raisins dried pineapple	2 liver 2 BY 1 vit C
6. Oats, pro, and nut butter, egg whites x 3, goats milk	2 liver 2 BY 1 vit C
	BCAA at bed

Different rep ranges

You may note that I have a vast array of rep ranges I use in my workouts.

When I was a young man I could just follow basic 5 to 8 rep sets most of the time and it worked very well increasing size strength and fullness.

As the years progress those lower rep ranges do not work as well when you have reached, or are near, your genetic potential.

Let's just say the fibre types for those reps are as big as they are going to get naturally and remember I am a natural for life guy.

By then you need to start looking at adding in many different rep ranges as there is much more to muscle size than just fibre thickness – there is capillary growth carb storage endurance fibres, sarcoplasm, and many other small things that add up to fullness and shape to the muscle.

So my goal is to keep some heavy work in, the basic moves but add to this lots of different stimulations that give me the look and feeling I want from my training. Fit, strong, agile and lean.

For instance, for the last few workouts leg sessions have been really high in reps.

Add to that lunges and high reps whereupon any legs have had a painful pump and legs have looked better and felt more pliable than usual.

I remember Vince Gironda, saying about Reg Park – that when he only did five rep sets he looked bulky and huge, and that it wasn't until he added other rep systems to his training that he took on the look of a champion.

Tuesday 31 March 2020

Up really early, even without work I still get up and have a fast walk for a few miles with the Doo.

Training

Rack shoulder press – this is in the rack, bench set at 80 degree - bar on pins at chin height. You press from a dead stop. Worked up after warm up.

Rack shoulder press   50kg x 5, 55kg x 5, 60kg x 5, 65kg x 5

Lat raise seated – touching dumbbells under hamstrings   12

Upright row   12, 3 times round

Incline curl – bench set at 80 degree, laid back on bench. Dumbbells at arm's length at sides and back. They stay back under no circumstances do you move elbows forward and engage the shoulders. This movement is awesome for a contraction at the top of the movement because you have altered the pull of gravity on the bicep. We super-set these with rope push downs.

Incline curl   12

Pushdowns   15 – 3 times round

Later I walked three miles with 16lb pack – could not do anymore police were about.

Then 300 lunges, then calves when I got home, 3 x 25. Band reverse curls, TNT bands, 3 x 15

Foods eaten

Food	Supplements
1. Eggs, cheese, oats, honey	2 liver, 1 Vit C, 2 Brewer's Yeast
2. Pro after training, banana	BCAAs
3. Bread – rye bread, peanut butter, yogurt	2 liver, 1 Vit C, 2 Brewer's Yeast
4. Oat cakes* I make	
	BCAA after lunges, calves, abs
5. Tuna, veg, and olive oil, potatoes	2 liver, 1 Vit C, 2 Brewer's Yeast
6. Muesli, granola, yogurt	
	BCAA at bed

*Oat cakes

8oz of oats

4 eggs

2 scoops protein - any flavour

2 handfuls of raisins

2 tablespoons honey

Smidge of water

Mix all together place in an oven-proof dish or tin, don't forget to grease the tin with coconut butter or butter. Cook on 180 for 30 or so minutes until brown.

Awesome for breakfasts or snacks. You can add bananas or berries to the mix, your choice.

Why I weigh myself every day

Something I very rarely did and only when I had to make a weight class or I was on a gaining program.

I weigh myself every day now to keep my weight the same. I am not counting calories, so I eat according to my morning weight, eat less if I go up, eat more if I go down that day.

It is a very simple way of balancing my body out.

My original goal was to weigh 145lb to powerlift so I was holding my weight there as that is the class I am in.

That's not going ahead now. But I am holding this weight as I feel very good at it.

Lean, muscular and very, very fit and agile.

The day

This morning saw the Black Kite again over my house. There used to be Red Kites about, don't know where they have gone, Red Kites are bigger, with a fork tail. Much bigger than the black at least five foot wing span.

Anyway the Black Kite was being chased of by 5 or 6 Crows, it must have been after a weak one.

As you can tell I love to see nature, I watched this for 5 or so minutes, so lucky to be close to nature.

I do miss the cabin though because we have not been able to go during the lockdown. Now that is in the wilds close to coast and close to miles and miles of open land.

We will soon be there I hope.

Plan is in the future when the kids need money for their own homes, to sell up here (Leeds) and head over to live in the cabin, Jo and I. The cabin is up the coast from Bridlington which was my hometown as a kid. So I have a deep connection with that area.

Wednesday 1 April 2020

First thing walked 2 miles no weight added.

Later five miles with 16lb pack on.

No running today or lunges as legs "mostly" tomorrow – did yoga at night for legs as well in order to make them nice and loose for tomorrow.

Foods eaten

Food	Supplements
Tea and honey	BCAA first thing
1. Oat cakes I made yesterday	2 liver, 1 Vit C, 2 Brewer's Yeast
2. Oat cakes again. Starving today.	2 liver, 1 Vit C, 2 Brewer's Yeast
3. Cottage cheese, mixed with nuts and raisins, this was a favourite of Steve Reeves, with Rye bread also and fruit.	2 liver, 1 Vit C, 2 Brewer's Yeast
I was starving when I got back from hike, lots of hills today with pack on.	
4 Nuts, fruit	
5 Tuna, rice, veg	
6 Yogurt and muesli	

Recovery work

I always know when my training is going well as I am starving hungry and have a really good appetite.

There has to be a balance of work and recovery work, one without the other won't have you making progress for long.

At present I am on a freestyle program as explained earlier and I am recovering very well from all I am doing.

One reason for this is I am not training as heavy as often and that does not break you or your system down as much.

You can do a shit load of lunges to a few sets of heavy squats, the heavy squats are going to break you down more. But this is what I am doing now – remember you need to chop and change programs the longer you have trained.

I will return to heavy stuff soon and I will build my recovery around it then - as for what I need at that point. I may just be able to hike and nothing else to aid recovery – maybe a bit of yoga.

But at the moment because the workouts (weights) are a "different" hard, I can do more "other stuff". I am still gaining, changing, and progressing in every area.

So what I am saying is back up your goal with the right recovery work. If you are getting ready for a show that is your goal, so you would not be doing loads of hill runs. You need all you have in the tank to do your show work. But walks, posing practice, and stretching will aid recovery. Maybe an afternoon nap every day. You need to build the perfect frame for you and your goal.

Thursday 2 April 2020

First thing 3 miles, later two miles.

Workout – duplicated a workout from 1995 when I was studying this journal for this book, wanted to see if I could still do it.

Yep -not far off at all. Back in the day at 30 I got 3 plates with wraps. No wraps today.

Training

Squat	2.5 plates a side	6
Leg extensions	45kg	15
Hacks	80kg	15
Front hacks	60kg	15
Then again		
Squats	2 plates a side	6
Leg extensions	45kg	15
Hacks	80kg	15
Front hacks	60kg	15

Leg curls	1 x 30
	1 x 6-8 heavy
	1 x 1 ½ reps - 1 full rep, and a ½ rep to fail
	5 sec hold in contraction point – each rep held contraction 5 seconds
	1 x negatives to fail, heavy, Jo lifted I lowered
	1 x medium reps to fail, normal set pumping, 20

Foods eaten

Food	Supplements
	BCAAs first thing
1. Oat scramble	2 liver, 1 Vit C, 2 Brewer's Yeast
2. Pro and carb drink needed it after workout	BCAAs
3. Bread – walnut and date, peanut butter, yogurt and fruit	2 liver, 1 Vit C, 2 Brewer's Yeast
4. Nuts, dried pineapple and raisins	2 liver, 1 Vit C, 2 Brewer's Yeast
5. Tuna, potatoes, veg	2 liver, 1 Vit C, 2 Brewer's Yeast
6. Muesli and goats milk	BCAA at bed
A few chocolates, that Louis had	

Today's workout was a killer. Not trained "bodybuilder style" for a long while now, like I was saying to Jo, you do not keep the size you once had when you come away from the intended goal, and in those days the goal was to be as big as I could be naturally and to be as ripped and conditioned as could be.

Every year – it was show after show – I must have done 80 or so – even more in all these years. Each year you planned assessed and strived to make improvements. If you had a weak point or points the idea was to improve them in the off-season and then turn up at the shows improved all ready for battle.

Today I proved only to myself, that I can still train hard. But not as often ha-ha. As recovery is not as good as we age.

I actually felt very fit today even though the workout was very fast and non-stop, my breathing was no problem at all. This has come from hiking and all the other "fast" work I do.

Sat here writing this I can feel my legs already and it feels good. Really enjoyed the session, as it was like going back in time. I even played the same music as back then, for that 45 minutes I was 30 again. And after I felt proud of myself – you have to be – you have to make the best of what you have and take positives from it all, and I know at 54 I am fitter than back then, maybe not as big, but that's all good. I'm happy with me of today.

Friday 3 April 2020, 145¾ - looking lean big and full, for me that is

Well I was right legs bloody sore today, but oddly I love it. Up early birds are singing. Let's have an awesome day.

Now going to try and walk these legs off a bit off out with Daisy Doo. 2 miles.

Later I did 5 then early evening another 2 to make my total for the day 9 miles. Legs felt much better for the day, I also did yoga to finish off the day at bedtime.

Foods eaten

Food	Supplements
	BCAAs
1. 3 eggs, hard boiled, cheese, rye bread and honey	2 liver, 1 Vit C, 2 Brewer's Yeast
2. Nuts and fruit	
3. Rye bread – cottage cheese, fruit	2 liver, 1 Vit C, 2 Brewer's Yeast
4. Nuts and dried fruit	
5. Tuna, veg, potatoes, and olive oil	2 liver, 1 Vit C, 2 Brewer's Yeast
6. Yogurt and granola	BCAA at bed

Up or down

You can see in the years gone by prior to shows. I keep and kept a detailed track of my food and calories.

These days after years of doing it I know instinctively how much to eat. So I eat just for the energy output I do. But what happens if I want to gain weight or lose it?

This again is a very simple process I have done myself and with clients for years.

First all we have to do is baseline your food each day. You don't even have to count calories. What I mean by a baseline is, same foods, same time same amounts every day. No changes.

Let's give you an "off the top of my head" baseline.

1. 3 eggs, 2 whole-wheat toast, small bowl of oats

2. 1 banana, 1 apple, 20 almonds

3. 1 tin of tuna, 1 large baked potato, dish of salad

4. 1 scoop of protein in water, 1 apple

5. 1 chicken breast, 1 cup of brown rice, 1 cup of vegetables

6. 1 pot (small) of yogurt

Two litre of water a day.

Simple – right all we do now is eat that day in day out for say 3 weeks.

Weigh yourself every couple of days, and if you do not deviate from the "baseline" your body will at first settle, then either balance you up a pound or two or lose a pound or two, just let it settle.

Let me say that the baseline has to be foods you like and baselined to your appetite.

The above is for a reference – for illustration purposes.

If you are wanting to get leaner after three weeks just chip away at your baseline. So on the above let's take away a few carbs to start with, just a smidge let's take away half the bowl of oats at breakfast and go to a medium potato at lunch. That will do for a couple of weeks or so. Then let's have a look at how things are going, keep training hard, maybe up your walks by a couple of miles a week.

By now you should have lost a little bit of bodyfat. So let's now chip away a bit more. Say take an apple off one of the snacks and go to half the cup of rice. Again that's all we need to do to keep taking off bodyfat steady without dropping the metabolism. Another few weeks might see us taking off 1 egg and a few almonds. This is a good calorie drop from fats not a huge amount but enough to kick in some more loss, along with hard training and staying active.

This simple process works really well no messing about counting stuff, just eat and do.

When you get to the weight/look you want simply add food back in the way you took it out. Eventually you can figure out foods you can eat and how much you can eat simply, like I can do, all it is, is being able to baseline things and keep notes, it's that simple.

The same can be done to gain weight – baseline and add little bits of food in, but remember the catalyst to it all is hard work in the gym, without the trigger of the gym nothing else will work as well.

Saturday 4 April 2020

First thing 2 mile walk.

Workout very good one with Jo and Lou.

Training

Exercise	Weight	Reps
Dumbbell incline press	25kg	12, 10, 8
Chins -wide grip right up to lower pec over bar		12, 10, 8
Flat dumbbell press	25kg	10, 10, 10
Bent over row – bent right over small plates on a bar, lowering bar right down, pulling with a shoulder width grip to lower pec. This really bites the upper lats.	50kg	12, 12, 12
Cross overs		15, 15
Pullovers	17.5kg	15, 15
Curls - bands		12, 12
Pushdown bands		15, 15

Foods eaten

Food	**Supplements**
	BCAAs first thing
1. 3 eggs soft boiled, cheese, oats, honey and cinnamon	2 liver, 1 Vit C, 2 Brewer's Yeast
2. Protein and carb powder after workout	BCAA
3. Rye bread, peanut butter, yogurt, banana	2 liver, 1 Vit C, 2 Brewer's Yeast
4. Chicken, lots of veg, potatoes, lovely meal Jo made – for Lou and I	2 liver, 1 Vit C, 2 Brewer's Yeast
5. Organic chocolate – cheat	
6. Granola, yogurt	
	BCAAs at bed

Super-sets, tri-sets

As you can see from my training logs, I use a lot of super-sets, tri-sets, and giant-sets, in my training.

Pretty much always have – even when doing lots of all body workouts the 9 to 12 exercises are done, bang bang bang one after another.

I have always been a big believer in getting the job done as fast as possible – not the reps mind you, but the workout as a whole.

I always work fast to increase the intensity of the workout.

Plodding from one exercise to another resting a set amount of time has never been my thing. I attack the muscle, hard and give it hardly any time to recover at all, hence super sets tri sets and the like. This way I can get a huge amount of work done in a short space of time, which is what I am after.

Other benefits apart from the intensity is increased cardiovascular effect, yes you are always in shape. I could never get my head round looking awesome – physique wise, but not being able to run up a flight of stairs.

For me - I want to be fit and healthy, this has always been more important to me than looks.

As you can see from the entries I combine antagonistic moves together, i.e. chest and back, biceps, triceps and I attack the same area but from different angles. Like a tri-set on legs for instance.

In the 1995 section of this book you can see that Jon and I did lots of tri sets and giant sets for legs. We changed the movements around a bit but always started with heavy squats and went right through all the moves non-stop. This was incredibly hard but the gains out distanced the pain. This was something I went back to year after year. Or a variation of it because it worked so well, because essentially you are doing 75 to 100 reps non-stop, and heavy weight, intensity was through the roof.

It was just the ticket for my skinny pins, they eventually became my best body part.

Sunday 5 April 2020

First thing 1 mile – beautiful day – sun is shining not a cloud in the sky.

Walk later with Jo, 5 miles.

Yoga at bed.

Foods eaten

Food	**Supplements**
	BCAAs first thing
1. 3 eggs, cheese, scrambled in olive oil	2 liver, 1 Vit C, 2 Brewer's Yeast
2. Fruit and walnuts	
3. Chicken rice, lots of veg	2 liver, 1 Vit C, 2 Brewer's Yeast
4. Tuna potatoes, lots of veg	2 liver, 1 Vit C, 2 Brewer's Yeast
5. Granola, yogurt, dried pineapple	
	BCAA at bed

The next six weeks

I/we tend to do programs in 6 to 8 week blocks.

I have found after 6 weeks or so there has to be some form of a change to the "stimulus" you are giving the body.

You start a new program, it takes a week or so to adapt a little, find your feet and start working hard. Then you see the fullness come, strength increase, maybe leanness coming through a bit more, i.e. you're changing. Then after so many weeks you don't look quite as good or feel as good, maybe you are just on the cusp of overtraining at that point. The routine change allows your body to take a step back then ramp up again.

Over the last 6 or 8 weeks we have been doing a freestyle routine sometimes all body sometimes a split, no set pattern at all. After training yesterday I stripped to a vest and was surprised by the size of fullness I had. You won't believe this but I do not have any full length mirrors in the house – so odd times I only see how I look in the gym. I am always wearing multiple layers anyway. Very rare do I wear a t-shirt or vest, it's just me.

I know that was as much as I am going to get out of the program we have been doing, or non-program and we need a change.

I spoke to Jo and Lou as Lou is training with us also and asked them what they wanted to do. Both are bodybuilding. Jo has a show at the year end and Lou is wanting to get bigger.

I'm easy as I can do all I need for hiking and fitness on other days, we decide to body-build.

So we came up with the next six weeks being a split program three days a week. As you can see through all of my career in bodybuilding I have done three days a week.

Then we will drop into a 6 week block of all body programs HIT style then a show prep for Jo.

The program here is a push and pull one.

I have done this many times back in the day. Heavily influenced by Lee Labrada – who I have kept extensive files on since I was a kid.

Day 1 – Chest shoulders triceps abs

Day 2 – Legs calves

Day 3 – Back bicep abs neck

Tuesday – Day 1

Thursday – Day 2

Saturday – Day 3

Other days for me, maybe Jo would be lunges, hikes, runs, maybe some drills or circuit work.

The bodybuilding days will be 6 to 9 sets for large body parts and 3 to 6 for small body parts. Rep ranges 6, 12, 15, 25 now all I am going to do is pull some moves from the exercise armoury at the front of this book.

This will give enough of a change each workout to make me ache like hell, always a good sign for me.

You will see how this pans out over this week, excited I always am with a new program.

Monday 6 April 2020, 146 feel really full and lean

First thing 1 mile.

Later 6lb pack did 5 miles with 5 hill sprints in it when I got back I was jigged. Just because it was so warm, I have got to start wearing shorts more whatever the weather, get my legs used to being out in all weather.

When I got back I had some BCAA and a meal and 10 – 20 minutes later I felt bang on again.

Foods eaten

Food	**Supplements**
	BCAAS first thing
1. Eggs x 3, Cheese, rye bread and honey	2 liver, 1 Vit C, 2 Brewer's Yeast
2. Nuts, walnuts, fruit	
3. Tuna, rice, lots of veg	2 liver, 1 Vit C, 2 Brewer's Yeast
4. Nuts, almonds, dates pineapple, raisins	BCAAs
5. Cottage cheese, baked potato, lots of veg	2 liver, 1 Vit C, 2 Brewer's Yeast
6. Yogurt and granola chopped banana also	
	BCAAs at bed

Protein

I have had years where I prepped for shows eating a fair amount of protein and some where I hardly ate any.

To be honest I looked better, performed better and felt better eating less. I think these days people are obsessed with protein intake counting every gram as if they will not gain an ounce of muscle if they are not eating a gram per pound, or two grams per pound of bodyweight. What they forget is, it's not the protein that makes you grow, it's the workout. The hard work, without that – the trigger, there is nothing, zilch. No stimulus, no gains. Eating protein will not make you have the body of your dreams, working hard will.

Look, eating protein is needed yes, but not in excess. I think eating a balanced healthy diet will do everything, yes everything for you as long as the training and recovery is on point.

I eat for health first and foremost. Yes I know back in the day I eat more protein than I do now, but that was only sometimes and I did not know any better. I have spent years studying nutrition and I mean 40 years of study and I eventually came to understand that health is first – not just looking good. Some competition bodybuilding diets I think are way off the mark in the health stand point. Also many of the fad diets are also unhealthy. Why? Because you restrict too many nutrients. We need a huge variety of foods for our health and to make sure we are awash with every vitamin and mineral and trace elements we need. You cannot get that from just eating lean meats and vegetables. We need everything.

So here's my take on protein. Yes eat some protein, complete protein you like in a day. It does not have to be a ton of it just don't fuss and eat some. Don't even count protein grams I keep things really simple, I eat in every meal – protein fats and carbs, every time I eat. When I say protein it maybe what's in a handful of nuts or what's in a yogurt or peanut butter.

I may have in a day real servings of protein twice, eggs at breakfast and then tuna at tea.

You can see from my food logs here it's not all chicken, beef, fish, turkey, egg whites, protein powder. Yes I may have a pro drink after a workout but I have more carbs than protein to be honest, I just call it pro drink out of habit.

Don't be a slave to this, it's simple, I am honestly as lean and as muscular at 54 as I ever was on just a lot of good wholesome nutritious foods. Nothing fancy at all, I just eat what's good for my health energy and wellbeing, and the muscle takes care of itself.

Tuesday 7 April 2020, 146 ½

First thing 2 mile walk.

Workout chest shoulders triceps, abs, new program

Training

Bench press – free not in rack	70kg	6, 6, 6
⌐ Incline flyes	17.5kg	12, 8, 8
└ Dips – no weight added, leaning forward to stress chest		8, 6, 6

Superset but non-stop back to back straight as I finished dips I went back to flyes

Standing press – hard after chest done	35kg	8, 8, 8
⌐ Lat raise seated	8kg	12, 12, 12
└ Upright row - superset	30kg	12, 10, 8
Push downs – kneeling down, rope	6 plates	15, 15, 15
Extensions bar	25kg	10, 10, 10
Abs – superset		
Crunch		20
Leg tucks		20, 3 times round

No other – activity today I did lots of writing and drawing

Foods eaten

Food	Supplements
	BCAAs
1. Eggs x 3, cheese, rye bread and honey	2 liver, 1 Vit C, 2 Brewer's Yeast
2. Pro, carbs after training	BCAAs
3. Rye bread, peanut butter, pear, yogurt	2 liver, 1 Vit C, 2 Brewer's Yeast
4. Nuts and dried fruit	
5. Tuna, rice, lots of veg and olive oil	2 liver, 1 Vit C, 2 Brewer's Yeast
6. Muesli and banana, yogurt	
	BCAAs at bed

Workout notes

Awesome workout – note different rep range, some straight sets some super sets – we did this with lots of focus, concentration and worked hard.

Will – stick to one basic move and change the others – so bench for chest and standing press for shoulders for a few weeks, chop and change on all other moves.

Let's give you a few tips.

Incline fly – bottom ¾ of movement, I always keep the dumbbells apart at the top to keep gravity on the muscle constant tension.

Dips – I have mentioned before, knees forward, elbows out to the side leaning into the move, it's a downward push, so the pecs do the brunt of the work.

Triceps extensions

A 6 inch between thumbs grip – thumbless grip – arms above the face at 75 or so degree backwards so the tension is on the arms. I bring the bar to the crown of the head and extend back up. Squeezing the triceps the bar always stays back over you never bring over your chest, there is no tension/gravity there.

Remember – feel the movement from A to B, squeeze the muscle always. Don't just do, do it right.

Notes on day

Enjoyed it even with the lockdown. Spent the day drawing and writing, had two commissions asked of me this week. Could get used to this work ha-ha.

Training was awesome, as above, also saw the black kite again god he's huge. Keep looking out for the red kites but not seen them in ages. They were reintroduced into the area a year or two ago, love love love being outside and seeing nature.

Wednesday 8 April 2020, 145 ½

Drop in weight as I knew it would, this was up a little for a few days, because I had meat here and there, I know it does not agree with my system these days, feel good today lean and mobile. Very high energy.

Spent the day writing and drawing again.

Later did two mile run and 5 x 10 crunch, 5 x 20 leg raise, 100 lunges.

Yoga at bed, ready for legs tomorrow.

Foods eaten

Food	Supplements
	BCAAs first thing
1. Eggs, cheese, rye bread, honey	2 liver, 1 Vit C, 2 Brewer's Yeast
2. Fruit and nuts	
3. Cottage cheese, raisins, dates, nuts, pineapple	2 liver, 1 Vit C, 2 Brewer's Yeast
4. Tuna, olive oil, rice, veg	2 liver, 1 Vit C, 2 Brewer's Yeast
5. Muesli, Goats milk	
	BCAA at bed

Notes on training

Forearms calves and neck

Just a few notes on key areas of the physique – I say key areas as neck is always on show, if you wear a shirt and have the sleeves rolled up even a baggy shirt you are portraying strength by having thick lean forearms.

Calves, no matter how big your quads are, if your calves are weak the whole leg looks weak.

If you compete, these areas along with the width of the shoulders and small waist make an awesome silhouette.

Neck

I have trained neck for years, the reason is when I am lean I loose size from there and it makes the whole upper body look "off". A strong neck adds to the thickness of the upper pecs, and also from the rear adds thickness to the traps which also adds quality and depth into back poses. Also as I have learned, it keeps my neck back and posture good, real strong, and mobile.

I do front flexion with a plate on my forehead laid on my back on a bench. Head off the end of the bench, a towel or something on the plate to protect my head. I open up my chin and stretch back and with the use of my neck muscles push the plate on my forehead to work the neck muscles.

The rear area I work with a neck harness, I have one from Ironmind that I have had nearly 30 years and it's still awesome. This I place on my head and bending over with a weight on the end of the harness, lift with the neck muscles at the rear of the neck. Try and incorporate some neck work in your program, go careful to start with, you can get very sore and hardly be able to move your head for days.

Forearms

Easy this one, I don't do much for them at all, only now and then do I work them. But here is my secret to big forearms – don't use straps!

If you grip everything while you are training and build grip strength, you will grow some forearms – it's that simple.

I deadlift, row, chin, with plenty of weight as should you and only use chalk to allow me to be able to grip the bar like a vice.

If you do this, in time you will have some chunky forearms. At first you are going to find it hard, but stick with it, one thing you will note is every time you train back your forearms will be sore. "Bingo" they will grow.

I noted when I was a kid, and doing the all body HIT training the grip really had to work, as the whole program is one thing after another no rest. My forearms blow up to the point I could never pull sleeves up. Kid you not.

Calves

A weak point for me for years I really had to work them in every different way to bring them up to win shows, years and years of thinking and trying.

My calves now are better than they have ever been, and here's why.

Hiking – I kid you not. They have really grown and are very lean, because of hiking. I think it's when I wear a pack it makes you lean forward a little and onto my toes. Plus all the hills I have done and uneven surfaces have stimulated them a lot.

Whenever I have hiked I have very sore calves – the next day.

All them years eh, ha-ha, I am so proud of my calves now I wear shorts ha-ha.

Another little trick I did because of the hiking thing was to work my calves in training free – i.e. not on a machine. I have machine at home, but thinking about how my calves have grown because of instability and balance I tried to work my calves just off a block about 4 inch high, holding a bar in front of me, as in the top of a deadlift. Then with balance raise up and down without the aid of anything to hold onto, the first time I did this for 3 x 25 my calves felt huge and sore for a few days, give it a try.

Thursday 9 April 2020

Up early, 2 mile walk.

Spent the morning drawing, two commissions to do, loved it.

Later trained legs, Lou spotted me, Jo a bit off today, not the virus just a bit overworked.

Training

Legs warm up.

Then squats 100 x 6, 120 x 6, 130 x 6, not powerlifting low but how I used to do them in my bodybuilding days

| Leg extensions | 45kg | 15 |
| Hacks | 100kg | 15, 2 rounds |

Calves, free as explained on Wednesday just 60lb 3 x 25

Foods eaten

	Food	**Supplements**
		BCAAs first thing
1.	Eggs x 3, oats, raisins, honey. Oats done as I call it Robby way (Robby Robinson), just pour on boiling water and leave to stand	2 liver, 1 Vit C, 2 Brewer's Yeast
2.	Pro carb after legs	BCAAs
3.	Nuts and fruit	2 liver, 1 Vit C, 2 Brewer's Yeast
4.	Tuna, lots of veg, boiled potatoes	2 liver, 1 Vit C, 2 Brewer's Yeast
5.	Cottage cheese, rice and lots of veg	2 liver, 1 Vit C, 2 Brewer's Yeast
	Cheat small piece of chocolate	
6.	Cheese and rye bread sandwich	BCAAs at bed

Iron in my blood

My love for exercise started at the age of 10 with press ups chins and running, and man could I run. I was not unlike Forest Gump. By 14 the iron bug had bit me with something that still burns hot today. Not once has it ever left me, I still love to train just like I did all those years back, same passion, same excitement same love.

Vince and I started training in the yard of his mum and dad's guest house, only a couple of blocks from the sea front.

We would train out in the sun with a home-made 60lb bar that was a couple of paint tins full of lead, scavenged off the beach. One man's loss was another man's gain. We melted down the lead into the two tins and shoved a bar into them, we used it for everything, I bet Vince still has it.

The sun would beat down on our wiry lean frames, as we pressed curled upright rowed and bench pressed on a wooden box.

Winter came and we set up the gym in the cellar. We had a mirror off a wardrobe, a blanket box for benching, a bull worker, chest expander and the bar. Pictures, stuck to the uneven white washed walls, Arnold, Franco, Coe, Zane, Danny, Robby, Lou, torn from Muscle and Fitness, stuck up with wall paper paste. We trained, we ran, we dug bait on the beach, we fished, we camped.

Life was simple but just the best. I had a broken home like so many, but my childhood was just awesome thanks to Vice's family who unofficially took me in.

By 16 I knew my life's passion and work, never had a doubt. I worked a few jobs to make ends meet and save but by my early 20s I was self-employed and earning a living from the sport I loved.

Over 30 years of working in the industry now and although I am semi-retired now, it's still awesome, still a buzz.

Training! Training will never stop, I will do it until my last breath that's when I will finish.

Friday 10 April 2020

Walked two miles first thing.

Lots of drawing again today, awesome day also. So spent most of it outside. Cannot bear being inside for long.

Later walked two miles, and did some yoga legs based as they were very sore.

Foods eaten

Food	**Supplements**
	BCAAs first thing
1. Muesli, granola, oats, fruit, goats milk	2 liver, 1 Vit C, 2 Brewer's Yeast
2. Fruit and nuts	
3. 3 eggs, cheese, rye bread, honey	2 liver, 1 Vit C, 2 Brewer's Yeast
4. Tuna, rice, veg	2 liver, 1 Vit C, 2 Brewer's Yeast
5. Muesli, goats milk	
	BCAA at bed

Saturday 11 April 2020

First things walked 2 miles.

Later 1 mile, later also 2 mile.

Not getting the miles in at the moment, been doing two commission drawings that take up hours each, need to have them done.

Training was ace, with Jo and Lou.

Training

Back and biceps

Chins	30kg	6, 6, 6
Deadlift and shrug, power shrugs	70kg x 8, 100kg x 8, 100kg x 8	
Bent over row	70kg, 80kg, 90kg	All 12
Curls	40kg	3 x 8
Seated dumbbell	20kg	2 x 12
Neck just did no rear as shrugs got that area, just front flexion plate on head	15kg	3 x 20

Yoga at bed

Foods eaten

Food	Supplements
	BCAAs first thing
1. Egg whites and banana(in notes)	2 liver, 1 Vit C, 2 Brewer's Yeast
2. Pro and carb drink after training	BCAAs
3. Oat cake as mentioned before	2 liver, 1 Vit C, 2 Brewer's Yeast
4. Chicken, potatoes, loads of veg	2 liver, 1 Vit C, 2 Brewer's Yeast
5. Tuna, veg, potatoes	
6. Oat cakes again	

Notes on day

So you have a week here of the new program. Five more weeks and we will then drop to a HIT all body. The constant change keeps my 43 year of training body, the change it needs to not regress and to keep in good shape all round.

Couple of moves you may not know

Deadlift shrugs – power shrugs

These I picked up years ago from Bill Star, it's a half deadlift in the rack, overhand grip – no straps – from just below the knee off the pins. Assume a deadlift stance, pull up as in a normal deadlift then forcefully – with power, shrug hard – a little like you would power clean but arms are out straight. Only a slight slight bend as in a normal shrug.

Smash up your traps hard into a powerful contraction.

Really good movement I used a lot back in 2007. For the Pro-Am and Worlds, really works all the backside of your body, from calves to the nape of the neck.

Bent over rows

Tight arch in the back I call it a in gorilla stance and with a shoulder width grip I pull the bar from past the knees to click my training belt buckle. Do not over swing these or lift up too far, it's called a bent over row for a reason!

Food

I wanted to cover some food here like I use to do back in the day. This is a bodybuilding way I don't follow as much now, I just eat healthy as you know.

But some of my early log books have these types of things and I wanted to give you the whys and wherefores.

Egg whites and banana on training days

I train early morning so after some BCAAs my first meal is just protein and some carbs, a light, easy digested meal with no fat added to it. The no fat added I will explain soon.

Six egg whites, one large banana with cinnamon

Whisk egg whites in bowl and chop in the banana, microwave 1.30 minutes

Take out, whisk again, cook again 1.30 minutes

Take out and whisk again.

It may need another 30 seconds or so.

Sounds awful, looks not great but is an awesome meal and I love it.

Now normally I eat protein fats and carbs in every sitting, but before a workout I want this to go into my system quick and be digested and utilised quickly. Adding fats to this meal would slow down the transit and digestion of the meal. I want to gain all I need from the meal, aminos into the blood, carbs to train and I want my system to be clear to except the protein and carb meal after training. The pro and carb drink now because I have had no fats the road is clear so to speak, so the carb and protein will be absorbed quickly, aiding recovery and necessary glycogen storage quickly. Quicker recovery quicker the gains.

This I did for years, and years with great gains. Afterwards about an hour later or so then have a "real" meal. In this case, I had oat cakes, made with full eggs, oats, raisins, protein powder. This added to the recovery of the system feeding the top up we had started with the protein carb recovery drink. Simple but effective.

I always liked training in the mornings and still do for the reason of recovery feedings. I could then feed the workout all day.

So let's recap

Meal 1 – protein, small carb serving, no fats

Train

Meal 2 – Protein and carb drink, and your supplements

Meal 3 – 1 hour after meal 2 – normal good clean meal comprising of protein, carbs and fats, i.e. chicken, rice, veg, olive oil

Back to the future

If you do not already I strongly urge you to keep a journal. I have journals from when I was 17 years old. I wish I had started them at 14.

I have done them every year since I always will, it is the most valuable book you will ever read because it's about you.

I learned from every book I have, it also makes me very proud to read them. I treasure them, always will.

I was talking to Jo today after we had trained hard and was eating one of our meals for the day. Chicken and potatoes, and loads of veg, along with the supplements for that meal.

Both of us said how simple a process this bodybuilding lark is if you just train hard. Hard and eat really good food, unfortunately people do not train hard enough, or consistent enough, let alone take time to prep their meals.

I don't believe in buying ready meals or having meals prepared for you, get bloody cooking, don't be a lazy so-and-so it's all part in parcel of looking after yourself.

Natural bodybuilding takes a long long time, you have to always be at the top of your game. You may not think it's worth it and that's okay each to their own.

I will always train and eat well its ingrained in me. It's not selfish, I train when others don't need me if that means 5am then so be it. I will never hurt others with my goals. Eating is just eating, everyone eats, I just won't eat crap in a meal. In a round-about way. I'm happy healthier and age better because of my choices this means I can be around and help others for longer.

I also just want to say, thank you for all the years of trust you have given me in helping you achieve your goals.

Please be the best you can be. If you can pass information onto others and inspire others with clean living, eating well and training hard, do so.

It's all about the lives we touch and help, this is how you live forever, in the minds and hearts of others.

Be the best you can be, and help others see what they can be also.

All the information here you have just read is from my journal of 2020 – it's been invaluable to me personally and I hope it's of value to you. If not now but as you age, snippets of information will be of use to you for life.

This has all been brought to you by me keeping a journal, start one now if you don't already log one, and make it a good ingrained habit for life.

Now let's pick up some of my journals from the past – these are old worn out dog eared, full of clippings and photos – cards from people or my kids. Just full of life from those years.

Following are years 1995 – the integral year for me as after winning the Novice British in 1988 this was my seventh attempt at winning the main title in the Mr Class. I kept coming close but it took 7 years of hard thoughtful work to pull it off.

You have 1995 – 2000 – 2007 – 2009 journals laid out in front of you. The years 1995, 2007, and 2009 will be of interest to the competitive bodybuilder looking to obtain a shredded condition. 2000 is a fantastic insight into getting as big and strong as possible. I will at the start of each journal give you the relevant information for that year.

Enjoy, absorb, pass on.

1995 BRITISH JOURNAL

Okay we have taken the Delorean to 88 miles per hour and we are screeching to a holt in 1995.

Louise and I owned Future Bodies Gym in Morley and were coming into our 5th year of the 16 years we had there.

I was just coming up to 30, and trained with still good mate Chris McHugh and John Torn for this show prep. Jon was featured in my last book under the chapter Brothers in Iron. Jon was and still is a very focused guy, we made a great team. As always Louise kept a keen eye on everything.

You may notice that there are no training activities the first week or two here as I was putting them into a different file at the time. But they appear in this journal a few weeks in, right up until the British.

I had in the past, a few times in my life bulked up to over 12 stone, after I came second at the Yorkshires this year to a very ripped Patrick Harris. I negatively decided I could not beat him at the British and just decided to get bigger. Then Louise give me a stern talking to, just 8 weeks out and told me to get my finger out and do the British or I would regret it. I lost nearly 2 stone in 8 weeks.

This year I trained with still good friend Jon Torn. We trained incredibly hard. Perhaps some of the most brutal workouts of my life. Jon placed second in the middleweights that year to the best natural bodybuilder from Britain ever Nigel Davis and I won the light weight class – beating Patrick and the winner from the year before.

Note also that the workouts here were built around hard contractions squeezing hard on each rep. Also a ton of stretching between sets, this is something I started in 93 with good results as I had all the John Parrello manuals and this is something I still do to this day.

Training like now was a little all-over the place – as I was training at my gym – that Louise and I owned Future Bodies Gym Morley, and training with Jon over in Doncaster – we just trained and when we met up decided what to "kill".

It worked very well and all body parts got done in a week – weaker ones more. I did also 2 sets of CV a day as I had weight to lose, years later I kept lean between shows I never had to do much, if any at all.

I was using AllSports Supplements at the time – as I stocked this in my gym, Jon also, it is still going today and one of my favourite companies in the World. They still do Amino Load by the way.

Enjoy these entries that were done 25 years ago, seems like yesterday.

Sunday 24 September 1995

		Cals	
08:15	Up, sunbed 20 minutes		
09:00	Eggs whites and banana	190	30
09:30	Oat cakes, 1 creatine	600	18
12:00	Chicken	180	30
	Spud	200	
12:30	Extra delts, calves, and twists for 10 minutes		
	30 minutes bike		
	Amino load and creatine, 4 Glutamine	150	
	Did some painting at gym, then home, 4 times round posing routine		
15:15	Chicken	180	30
	Spud	200	
	Veg, salad, just plain salad	40	
	Lemon tea		
	Sunbed and more posing comparisons this time		
	Went to pictures to see Apollo 13, very good		
	Apple	60	
20:00	At home fish	166	36
	Veg	50	
22:30	Fish	166	36
	Veg	50	
			180
	Wine	70	
		2302	

Look a lot sharper and fuller happy so far

Steaks knocked on the head now fish on Sat for the next few weeks, should get loads tighter from now on

Photo by Robert Logan

Monday 25 September 1995, 11 stone 2

		Cals	
06:30	Up sunbed 15 minutes		
	Louise still in kip had to wake her to make my eggs or else		
07:00	Egg whites and banana	190	30
08:00	Gym bike 15 minutes and stepper 15 minutes		
09:00	Oat cakes	600	15
11:00	Chicken	180	30
	Spud	200	
	Workout with Jon, back and triceps, and half hour bike again (killer)		
	No twists today give abs a rest for big whack tomorrow		
14:00	Chicken	180	30
	Spud	200	
	Went home sunbed 20 minutes and practiced posing, 4 times each, quarter turns and compulsories		
16:00	Gym		
17:00	Fish	164	36
	Veg	100	
19:45	Tuna	100	20
	Veg	50	
22:30	Fish	168	36
	4 Rice cakes melon and tea	120	197
		2252	

Nothing with last meal my belly full of wind

Walk 20 min at night, 4 times round posing routine

4 Glutamine before bed

No steaks now, last 3 meals veg and no starchy carbs, weight around 11 stone 2, in morning 11:00

Good day all went well

Tuesday 26 September 1995

		Cals	
06:30	Up sunbed 20 minutes		
	Bath and shave		
07:15	Eggs and banana	190	30
08:00	Gym, 15 minutes stepper 15 minutes bike		
	Abs with Louise		
09:15	Oat cakes	600	15
11:30	Chicken	180	30
	Spud	200	
	Tired and irritable today		
14:00	Chicken	180	30
	Spud	200	
14:30	Went home, 4 times routine 4 times compulsories, quarter turns, sunbed 20 minutes		
	Bath and shave		
16:00	Back at gym felt much better		
	Apple	60	
	Amino load and creatine	150	
17:30	Fish	164	36
	Veg	70	
19:45	Tuna	100	20
	Veg	50	
	Busy at gym tonight had to do most of the cleaning on my own, no staff		
19:30	Walk home 25 minutes fast in boots		
	Killed my calves		
22:15	Fish	200	40
	Veg		
	Melon		
	Lemon tea	2344	201
	Look a lot tighter tonight, things coming together		

Wednesday 27 September 1995, 11 stone and half a pound

		Cals	
06:30	Up sunbed 20 minutes		
07:15	Eggs and banana	190	30
	Walk to gym half hour, twists 10 minutes		
09:00	Oat cakes	600	15
	Had a good clean round gym		
11:15	Chicken	180	30
	Spud	200	
13:30	Chicken	180	30
	Spud	200	
14:00	Home sunbed 20 minutes		
	Posing practice		
15:15	Back at gym		
	More abs, side crunches and side cable crunches		
	Shoulders (great one) calves good, bike half an hour		
	Amino load and creatine	150	
15:15	Fish	164	30
	Veg	50	
19:30	Tuna	100	20
	Rice cakes	120	
21:15	Pose routine 4 times		
21:30	Left gym		
21:45	Half hour walk		
	Bath and shave		
23:00	Fish	170	36
	Veg	100	
	Melon	20	
	Had creatine in Amino load and 4 glutamine after workout and 4 before bed	2424	191
	Looking sharpish now		

Thursday 28 September 1995

		Cals	
06:30	Up and sunbed 20 minutes		
	Eggs and banana	190	30
	No aerobics this morning		
08:00	Oat cakes	600	15
08:45	Set off to Jon's. Trained at Dayo's in Doncaster good workout. Chest and abs.		
	Went to see Edna Taylor had a look at her gym, okay, she is nice		
12:30	Chicken	180	30
	Spud	150	
	Oops forgot Amino Load and creatine after workout	150	
	Went for fast walk with Jon half hour at least, plus some step work on railway bridge		
	Killer 45 minutes total		
14:15	Chicken	180	30
	Spud	200	
16:30	Bike 20 minutes twists 10 minutes		
17:30	Home		
	Fish	170	36
	Veg	100	
	Went to Thunder concert in York not as good as in Bradford – acoustics better in Bradford at St George's Hall		
	2 apples	120	
23:00	Tuna	100	20
	Veg	100	
		2240	161
23:45	Home		
	Creatine and glutamine		
	Freezing cold when got home look sharp though		
	No posing tonight no walk, done enough today		
	Back to it tomorrow		
	Abs before bed and bike after legs and walk at night, posing in morning after lay in		

Friday 29 September 1995

		Cals	
06:30	Up Eggs and banana	190	30
	Back to sleep		
10:00	Oat cakes	600	15
	Up sunbed 20 minutes		
	Posing practice		
	Cook food for day		
12:00	Chicken	180	30
	Spud	250	
	Back to gym (creatine) 1 spoon		
13:30	Abs and twists		
14:00	Chicken	180	30
	Spud	100	
14:30	Leg workout (killer again)		
	Bike half hour		
	Amino load and creatine 2 spoons		
17:00	Fish	170	36
	Veg	50	
19:30	Tuna	100	20
	Veg	50	
	Apples through day	120	
22:45	Fish	170	37
	Melon	20	
	Wine	70	
			198
	2 rice cakes	60	
		2310	

Posing practice before last meal and half hour walk

Still look sharp abs look better today

4 glutamine before bed and 4 after workout also

5 Aminos with each meal

1.5 litre of water

Note – I was having 3 carb based meals early in the day here, oat cakes, chicken and potato for 2 meals, then 3 meals of fish and vegetables. This was to keep carbs early in the day near my workouts. It worked very well.

Simple – it was so simple – Chris still talks about it to this day, he calls it "chicken spud – chicken spud – fish veg diet".

Saturday 30 September 1995

No more raisins or apples now too simple a sugar keep bananas and melon in though, for breakfast will mix my oats with shreddies and banana and make oak cakes out of that.

		Cals	
07:30	Up Eggs and banana	190	30
	Sunbed 20 minutes		
	30 minute walk to gym		
09:30	Oats and shreddies and banana	663	26
10:30	Abs and twists just sides today, side bends and cable side crunch		
11:30	Chest and biceps 20 minutes bike		
13:00	Chicken	180	30
	Spud	200	
	Carbo load after workout and 1 creatine	150	
16:00	Spud	200	
	Chicken	180	30
	Around town and to Martyn's		
	Also went for a stand-up sunbed 6 minutes (good)		
20:00	Meal out Milwaukee Diner steak	500	50
	Veg and salad	100	
	Wine and loads of coffee		
22:30	Fish	170	37
	Veg	50	
	Melon	30	
		2613	203

Walk half hour before last meal and posing routine also did compulsories before going out

8 Glutamine before bed

Sunday 1 October 1995, 10 stone 13

		Cals	
07:30	Up sunbed 20 minutes		
08:00	Eggs and banana	190	30
08:30	Gym extra delts and forearms, also abs.		
	3 giant sets, bike 20 minutes, twists 10 minutes, 1 spoon creatine		
	Very busy in gym taking people round missed a meal		
11:00	Oat cakes	663	21
13:00	Chicken	180	30
	Spud	200	
14:30	When done at gym went to Roundhay Park, 45 minutes aerobics, stairs and walking		
16:00	Amino load and creatine	150	
17:00	At home chicken	180	30
	Spud	150	
	Veg	50	
	Cup of herbal tea (nice)		
	Practiced routine then sunbed 20 minutes and posed again, 4 times round. Look a lot sharper still a bit on abs and lower back but still look very full. 3lbs off should do it nicely now just get ripped.		
19:30	Fish	170	36
	Veg	50	
	2 wines through night	140	
22:30	Fish	170	36
	Veg	50	
	Melon	50	
		2393	183

Monday 2 October 1995 back to it, 3 weeks to go

		Cals	
	After a nice night relaxing with the wife feel great today full of energy and alive		
06:30	Sunbed 20 minutes		
07:00	Eggs and banana	190	30
08:15	Gym, stepper 15 minutes, 10 minute twists, side bends and cable side crunches		
09:15	Oat cakes with shredded wheat	663	21
	Workout back 10 sets chins different widths and grips 12 to 8 reps per set		
	Bent over rows I worked on 3 x 8, 10 reps		
	Squeezing hard, shrugs 3 sets		
	Triceps close grip smith press and pushdowns, and kickbacks. Bike 20 minutes, Amino load and creatine, shower	150	
11:30	Chicken	180	30
	Spud	200	
	Had a good clean out in back way and round gym		
14:30	Chicken	180	30
	Spud	200	
	Home for a sunbed 20 minutes and posing practice 4 times round each plus 6 x 10 second squeezing on thighs. Need more separation in hamstrings. Do extra work for them tomorrow		
17:30	Fish and veg	170	36
20:00	Pro mix	50	
	2 rice cakes	140	15
		60	
22:45	Fish	170	36
	Melon	20	
		2373	198

Half hour walk and posing practice

Start on extra Aminos in between meals now

Tuesday 3 October 1995

		Cals	
06:30	Up sunbed 20 minutes quick shower	190	30
07:00	Eggs and banana		
07:30	Gym Bike and stepper total 30 minutes		
	Abs and twists, 1 spoon creatine		
09:00	Oat cakes	663	21
	Did some odd jobs in gym		
11:30	Spud	200	
	Chicken	180	30
13:30	Chicken	180	30
	Spud	200	
	Workout delts with Joh very fast, and great pump. Bike half an hour level 3, shower and coffee		
	Amino load and creatine after workout	150	
	Went home about 4ish posing 4 times round, and 6 leg squeezes, crunch 10 seconds each		
17:30	At gym fish	170	37
	Veg	100	
	Very busy in gym		
20:00	Tuna	100	20
	Veg	50	
21:45	Home, posing 3 times, walk 20 minutes		
11:00	Fish	170	37
	Melon	50	
		2403	205

Coffee

4 glutamine before bed

Look sharp now still a little on lower back and biceps and rear delts and hams, 2 – 3 will make the sharpest ever

Wednesday 4 October 1995

		Cals	
06:30	Up sunbed 20 minutes quick shower		
07:00	Eggs and banana	190	30
07:45	Arrive at gym		
	Bike half hour read a batman graphic novel very good, half hour to read it, twists		
	Side abs dumbbell 3 x 20 3 x 20 cable side crunch		
	Spotted Mark for delts, did calves and forearms		
10:30	Amino load with 2 spoons creatine	150	
11:30	Chicken	180	30
	Spud	200	
	Did odd jobs and made some phone calls, pushed Janine through workout, wiped round		
14:15	Chicken	180	30
	Spud	200	
	Went home around 3ish came back no key. First real tantrum went mad (silly sod)		
15:30	Sunbed 20 minutes posing practice 4 times round each really hard squeezing sides coming out more still very full happy. Creatine when got back.		
17:30	Fish	170	36
	Veg	100	
20:00	Tuna	100	20
	Veg	50	
21:40	Knacked tonight feel very tired. Home pose 3 times routine walk half an hour, bath and shave		
10:45	Fish	170	37
	Melon	50	
	Look very tight tonight		
	Oops forgot oat cakes	663	183
		2403	

Thursday 5 October 1995

		Cals	
06:30	Up sunbed 20 minutes		
07:00	Eggs and banana	190	30
07:50	Gym Oats and shreddies	663	21
	Put Ian through a chest and triceps workout		
10:45	Chicken	180	30
	Spud	150	
11:00	Workout with Jon chest abs, and bike half an hour. Twists 10 minutes stepper 10 minutes		

Went and got my hair cut very very short, Louise said I look a prat but I want a different look for show. Smaller head and wider shoulders.

This was the first time since I was 10 or so I had had a crew cut. From this point on I had a crew cut as soon as I started prep for other shows. It became a tradition, Louise never did like it but put up with it ha-ha.

	Amino load plus creatine	150	
14:15	Chicken	180	30
	Spud	200	
	Come home sunbed 20 minutes 4 times round		
	Posing creatine and spud	100	
	Back at gym put Louise through legs		
17:00	Fish	170	37
	Veg	100	
20:00	Tuna	100	20
	Veg	100	

Robin Story from AllSports Supplements called with supplements he gave me a sweat shirt (great) and loads of freebies looks after us, very much so.

21:45	Home, 3 times routine		
22:00	20 minute walk		
22:45	Fish	170	37
	Melon	50	
		2503	225

Good day felt full of energy all day very productive day got lots done and sowed a lot of seeds in the gym

4 glutamine after workout

4 before bed

6 October 1995 – Friday thank God

		Cals	
06:30	Up sunbed 20 minutes		
07:00	Eggs and banana	190	
	Gym, did bits and bobs		
09:00	Oat cakes	663	21
09:30	Workout legs		
	Squats 3 plates, leg extension, hacks, front hacks, and squats 2 plates on second round. 2 Giant sets.		
	Hams, leg curls 6 sets. 1 light 30 reps. 1 heavy 6 reps with F&N. 1 and ¼ reps, 1 hold for 5 seconds at top, 1 negs 6 – 8, 1 to fail medium weight.		
	Lunges up gym 10kg twice (killer). Bike half hour abs before workout just sides, bends, crunches, side cable		
	Twists 10 minutes – Amino load and creatine, 2 spoons	150	
11:30	Chicken	180	30
	Spud	200	
14:30	Home chicken small	100	25
	Spud	200	
	Back to gym creatine 1 spoon		
17:00	Fish	170	37
	Veg	100	
	Very very busy in gym, legs killing me as well		
20:00	Tuna	100	20
	Veg	80	
21:45	Home. Pose 3 times did other's today at home. 4 times round.		
	Walk half an hour, look very tight tonight shoulders and chest still very full creatine is great and glutamine. Louise and I decided not to weigh myself any more just go by how I look from now get see through skin and as full and as veiny as poss so they say what has Duckett done this time to look like that		
	Fish	170	37
	Melon	50	
	Wine	70	
		2423	170

4 glutamine after workout

4 before bed

Saturday 7 October 1995, still 1.5 litre water a day

		Cals	
07:30	Up eggs and banana, 20 minutes sunbed	190	30
09:30	Gym, oat cakes	663	21
10:15	After a few jobs		
	Abs, crunches on roman chair superset with leg raise incline, twists 10 minutes		
	Biceps Platz dumbbell curls*, 5 sets to fail		
	Bike half an hour		
12:00	Spud	200	
	Fish	170	37
15:10	In town, chicken	180	30
	Spud	200	
	Went to Makro and dropped off at gym		
18:00	Home Chicken	180	30
	Veg	100	
	After sunbed and posing, Louise put me through it. Said 90% there a lot tighter in back and lower chest line (still full happy)		
19:15	Pictures Assassins Sly Stallone, good film. Louise ate some sweets.		
22:00	Home walk half an hour after 3 times routine		
23:00	Fish	170	37
	Melon	100	
	After workout today Amino Load and creatine	150	
	Plus creatine 1 spoon before bed, posing and also 4 glutamine after workout and 4 before bed		
		2303	185

*Platz Dumbbell Curls are seated back on a high incline bench. Curling both together until fail then sit up off the incline (sat upright now) curl again until fail, both arms together. Then do one arm at a time curling one dumbbell you will find you can still do some – 2 or 3 each side, when that fails just do short twists at the bottom – I saw Platz do this years ago when Louise and I were in California.

Sunday 8 October 1995

		Cals	
07:30	Up, eggs and banana	190	30
	At gym side abs, twists 10 minutes, side bends, 3 x 20, cable crunches 3 x 20		
	Delts lat raise with squeeze and twist of elbows super set with press behind neck with a hard contraction at top, 3 sets each (killed) stretched and posed in-between each set. Hard		
	Calves standing, 16 plates 10 – 12 reps with hard squeeze and shit* squat calves 10 – 12 reps. Stretch and pose in-between each set		
	Going to stretch and pose a lot in-between each set from now until show and bring in even more detail, killed when did it today		
09:35	Oat cakes	663	21
	Amino load after workout and creatine	150	
12:30	Chicken	180	30
	Half a spud	100	
14:30	Went to Roundhay Park again up and down stairs 10 times walk 15 minutes, 40 minutes total		
15:15	Chicken	180	30
	Rice cakes x 3	90	
16:30	Home Coffee and supplements		
	Posing routine sunbed and compulsories.		
	Chill out rest of night have bloody earned it this week		
18:15	Fish	170	37
	Veg	80	
	Two wines tonight	140	
22:00	Fish	170	37
		2113	185

8 glutamine before bed

Look a lot tighter and fuller cannot believe my chest size difference things going well more posing these next few weeks to get freaky.

*Shit squat calf raise are a move by Parrillo. Holding a weight upright, squat down and do a free hand seated calf raise. Look up Parrillo and calf training, very good movement.

Monday 9 October 1995 – water packed tuna from now

		Cals	
06:15	Up sunbed 20 minutes, eggs and banana	190	30
07:40	Gym bike 20 minutes, abs 3 giant sets, hyper, crunch, leg raise and hip flex		
08:40	Oat cakes	663	21
09:15	Workout back, chins 3 sets 20kg and 25kg, with pullovers, stretching and squeezing, and posing in-between		
	Each set lat spreads and double biceps		
	Pulldowns 2 sets 75 – 80kg to fail stretching and posing again. Low pully 2 sets to fail again stretch and pose		
	Bent over rows light, 1 plate each side, with dumbbell rows together 10 – 12 reps each to pump, stretch and pose, each set		
	Triceps lying extensions 15kg each side, 2 x 8 10 reps		
	Seated overhead extension 2 x 8 reps. Pushdowns 2 sets, stretch and pose. Kickbacks pump set 5kg 2 x 20 each, stretch and pose		
	Very very good workout killed me posing		
	Bike 20 minutes and twist 10 minutes		
11:15	Spud	150	
	Chicken	180	30
14:00	Spud	200	
	Chicken	200	
	Sups after workout Amino load and creatine	150	
15:30	Home posing and sunbed, very hard posing session		
	1 spoon creatine when got back		
17:00	Fish	170	37
	Veg	80	
20:00	Tuna water packed	100	20
	Veg	50	
23:00	fish	170	37
	Melon	100	
		2403	205

Half an hour walk and 3 times routine

Look very tight now just a bit on lower lats to go and legs water to come off will be spot on

Tuesday 10 October 1995

		Cals	Pro	Carbs
06:30	Up, not a very good night's sleep only about 3-4 hours			
	Sunbed 20 minutes, shower and shave			
	Eggs and banana	190	30	20
07:50	Gym, bike half an hour reading Parrillo book			
	Side ab work, side bends and cable crunches side 3 x 20 each, twists 10 minutes, some stretching for legs			
09:15	Oat cakes	663	21	112
	Half amino load with 3 creatine, in other half in afternoon after posing	150		80
11:30	Chicken	180	30	
	Spud	150		30
14:30	Chicken	180	30	
	Spud	200		30
14:45	Bike 20 minutes felt like doing more, very, very psyched for show			
	Home sunbed 20 minutes and posing very hard squeezing			
17:00	Back at gym, fish	170	36	
	Veg	80		5
20:00	Tuna in water	80	20	
	Veg	80		5
	(20 minutes' walk and pose)			
23:00	Fish	170	37	
	Melon last bit	100		5
	1 lemon tea – no sorry just a herbal tea			
		2393	204	287

8 glutamine before bed

Look very tight tonight veins everywhere happy, keep at it

Decided to knock fruit on head now 10 days to go to get last bit off abs and lower chest and back. It will knock out 200 calories or so.

Wednesday 11 October 1995

		Cals	Pro	Carbs
06:30	Up sunbed 20 minutes			
	Eggs x 6 with mushrooms (bloody awful)	90	30	
07:50	Gym, abs rope crunches 10 x 20 reps			
	Twists 10 minutes			
09:00	Oat cakes	565	21	92
	Did some bits and bobs,			
11:00	Meal chicken	180	30	
	Spud	200		30

*Workout with Jon Torn last leg one, killer

Squats 3 plates 6 to 8 reps, leg extensions, hacks, then sissy hacks, roman chair. 2 giant sets 2nd set 2.5 plates on squats

Leg curls 6 sets, 1 high reps, 1 heavy F&N (forced reps and negatives)

1 - 1 ¼ reps, 1 negs, 1 holding 5 seconds at top

1 to fail, lunges 2 times up and down gym

Hypers 2 sets really squeezing

In-between each set stretch and pose

Bike half an hour (killer workout)

Got butterflies before felt sick in-between

Happy when done, read Platz book before helped – visualised and very focused

		Cals	Pro	Carbs
	Amino load and creatine	150		80
15:00	Home posing and sunbed			
17:00	Fish	170	37	
	Veg	80		5
20:00	Tuna in water	100	20	
	Veg	80		5
	Home 3 times routine walk 1 hour			
23:00	Fish	170	37	
	Herbal tea			
	Chicken breast	180	30	
	Look tight and still full	1965	205	212

*I would – and did all my years from then on, do my last leg workout 10 days out. This would bring my legs in much harder, I also passed this on to clients over the years, always 100% success rate.

Thursday 12 October 1995

		Cals	Pro	Carbs
06:30	Up sunbed 20 minutes, eggs, mushrooms, tomatoes	90	30	
07:50	Gym bike half an hour, side abs and twists 10 minutes			
09:00	Oat cakes 1 spoon creatine	565	21	92
	Did some bits and bobs round gym			
11:00	Chicken	180	30	
	Spud	150		30
13:00	Went home for a few hours with our lass nice surprise Tom Platz book came great			
	Sunbed and posing very hard, look tight and arms stuck on now, veins everywhere			
14:30	Chicken	180	30	
	Spud	150		25
17:00	Back to gym, fish	170	37	
	Veg	80		5
	Extra chicken for fruit calories	180	30	
	Veg	50		5
	Good night in gym, Robin came with supplements			
	Home pose and walk half an hour			
	Tried tan on Louise said no good take her word for it, she's been right so far this time			
23:00	Fish	170	37	
		1965	215	157

Herbal tea

Look sharp lads had a look at me at gym said I have never been sharper or fuller

8 glutamine before bed

Friday 13 October 1995, 9 days to go

		Cals		Carbs
06:15	Up quick shower and eggs	90	30	
	½ oat cakes ½ after workout	563	21	92
07:40	Workout chest and shoulders with Phil			

Incline dumbbell press 35kg 8 to 10 reps just ¾ movement bottom part felt it more, bench press 1 plate plus 15kg 6 – 8 reps to fail - 3 ¾ movement again flyes same again 2 sets 27.5kg, 7 reps

Cross overs 2 x 25 reps

Smith press 10kg a side no lock-out, 2 x 6 – 8 reps, lat raise 2 drop sets

Bent over lat raise 2 sets to fail

Abs 3 giant sets side bends, 2 x 100 reps 5kg crunch – leg tucks

		Cals		Carbs
	Bike 30 minutes (great workout) amino load and creatine	150		80
11:30	Chicken	180	30	
	Spud	180		30
13:00	Home sunbed 20 minutes and posing			
14:30	Chicken	180	30	
	Spud	150		30
17:30	Fish	170	37	
	Veg, 1 spoon creatine	50		5
10:00	Tuna	100	20	
	Veg	50		5
10:45	Fish	170	37	
	Chicken	180	30	
		2213	205	242

Herbal tea

Look very sharp tonight chest killing already from this morning and I am shagged out tonight. Half hour walk and posing

8 glutamine before bed

Photo by Robert Logan

Saturday 14 October 1995, 8 days to go

		Cals	Pro	Carbs
	½ gram of extra vit C each meal and 1 spoon extra creatine, 4 a day now			
06:15	Up quick shower and eggs, coffee	190	30	
07:15	Gym half an oat cake before workout and after	563	21	92
07:30	Arms triceps lying extensions 20kg each side 2 sets 8 or so reps on own 2 forced, overhead extensions 10kg each side 2 sets 10 to 12 reps, pushdowns just bottom part full stack 8 to 10 reps			
	Biceps 3 sets incline curls 20kg to fail. 6 to 4 reps 2 – 3 forced. 10kg last set to burn out			
	Bike half an hour, side bends 200 reps each side and hanging leg raise 2 sets to fail			
	Must have forgot Amino Load always have it after workout			
	Shower and shave felt good then, legs looked very tight in changing rooms veins all over them I was very surprised myself, never never seen them like this. Fingers crossed my year this year.			
11:00	Chicken	180	30	
	Spud – lemon tea bag	150		30
14:00	Chicken	180	30	
	Spud	150		30
	Into town, coffee small			
17:15	2 creatine			
17:45	Fish	170	37	
	Veg small coffee	50		5
20:15	Tuna	100	20	
	Veg – lemon tea small cup tea bag	50		5
	Watched Dumb & Dumber again (good)			
	Wine	70		2
23:00	Fish	170	37	
	And Chicken	180	30	
		2203	235	164

Stairs at Roundhay and walk at night 20 – 25 minutes

Last aerobics thank god

Make notes of all coffee's now, 1.5 litre water a day as well

8 glutamine at bed

Sunday 15 October 1995, 1 week to go. Still 1.5 litre water a day

		Cals	Pro	Carbs
07:00	Up, eggs 1 small coffee	90	30	
08:00	Gym abs, hyper, crunch, leg raise and hip flex, 3 giant sets			
	Side bends 2 x 100 reps and hanging leg raise			
	Calves, 6 sets, 1 high reps, 1 heavy 6 to 8, 1 ½ reps, 1 negs, 1 - 5 second hold, 1 high rep to fail			
09:00	Oat cakes (1 large coffee Atlanta mug*)	563	21	92
11:15	Chicken	180	30	
	Spud (1 small lemon tea 1.2 Atlanta mug*	150		30
	Oops forgot amino load after workout 2 creatine	150		80
	*Gary and Steve had a look at me today both said they were impressed, Gary told me to keep everything the same no changes in food this week and water keep going			
14:15	Chicken (1 small coffee)	180	30	
	Spud	150	30	
14:45	Posing and sunbed 25 minutes and more posing, then shave all my bits for show time and a good scrub, then 2 creatine, look bloody white now I have had a skin scrub			
17:00	Fish, 1 small coffee	170	37	
	Veg	80		5
20:00	Tuna, 1 lemon tea small	100	20	
	Veg	80		5
	Wine while watching Nell movie	70		3
22:30	Fish	170	37	
	Chicken grilled	180	30	
		2313	235	245

20 minutes' walk could not resist it

8 glutamine before bed

*Atlanta mug was a coffee cup I got from "Atlanta" – ha-ha this I used as a measure of coffee so I knew what I was taking in. It was a huge thick white American mug, god I loved that mug. Ha-ha.

*Gary Thornton – still a real good friend to this day. Gary said – if I changed anything he would beat the hell out of me – ha-ha.

This also stood me in good stead for years to come competing, as when you are ready don't change a thing and ruin the whole process, thinking you are going to magically improve. Secret is get sharp and hold it.

The longer you hold it the harder you will become. Stick to the plan and cruise into the show. No carbing up, no dropping water, just diet, get ready weeks before and hold it. Simple.

Monday 16 October 1995, count down 6 days

		Cals	Pro	Carbs
06:00	Up sunbed 20 minutes, eggs, 1 small coffee	90	30	
07:30	Gym, back, low pully rows 2 sets 80kg to fail			
	Pullovers across bench 35kg 2 sets to fail			
	V bar chins 2 sets to fail, with half plus ¼ reps			
	Abs roman chair and side bends, 3 sets			
	2 times round posing (look very good today keep everything the same this week spot on)			
	Amino load and creatine	150		80
08:30	Oat cakes, 1 large coffee Atlanta mug	563	21	92
	Did some jobs			
11:00	Chicken, 1 small lemon tea, half Atlanta mug	180	30	
	Spud	170		30
	More jobs			
13:00	Went home 2 x round posing, sunbed			
14:15	Chicken, 1 small coffee	180	30	
	Spud, 2 creatine	150		30
14:15	Chicken, 1 small coffee	180	30	
	Spud, 2 creatine	150		30
17:00	Fish, 1 small coffee	170	37	
	Veg	80		5
	Very very busy day in the gym			
09:30	Walk 20 minutes, 3 times routine, plus 2 times round posing			
22:30	Fish, 1 small lemon tea	170	37	
	Chicken	180	30	
		2413	245	267

Look very very sharp tonight, striations in triceps and chest like never before, happy

8 glutamine before bed

Tuesday 17 October 1995, still 1.5 litre water

		Cals	Pro	Carbs
06:15	Up, sunbed 20 minutes, eggs	90	30	
07:30	Gym, Shoulders, smith standing press			
	3 sets to fail, ½ and ¼ reps			
	Lat raise one arm drop sets 2 each, 15kg, 10kg, 7.5kg to fail, ½ and ¼ reps			
	Amino load and creatine	150		80
	Side abs, bends and cable crunches, 2 times posing			
08:30	Oat cakes	563	21	90
	Went into town Martyn's, picked up some bits and bobs			
11:00	Chicken, 1 small lemon tea	180	30	
	Spud	150		30
13:00	Home, 3 times routine, sunbed 20 minutes, 2 round posing			
	Cook some food for tomorrow			
14:30	Chicken, 1 small coffee	180	30	
16:00	Spud, 2 creatine	150		30
16:45	Fish, 1 small coffee	170	37	
	Veg	80		5
19:45	Tuna, 1 small lemon tea bag, Atlanta mug	100	20	
	Veg	80		5
21:40	Home, walk 20 minutes 2 times posing and bath			
22:45	Fish, 1 small herbal tea	170	37	
	Chicken	180	30	
		2243	235	240

Look very tight tonight still full as well, sides come in more and lower back, legs have veins in them when warm loads in abs as well

8 glutamine before bed

Wednesday 18 October 1995

		Cals	Pro	Carbs
	*1 cup lemon			
07:30	Up, today felt much better for lie in			
	Eggs, 1 small coffee	90	30	
08:15	Gym, abs, crunches, leg raise and side work			
09:00	Oat cakes, 1 large coffee	563	21	90
	Hair cut			
11:00	Workout last one – 3 bicep curls			
	Chest incline dumbbell press, up to 40kg forced reps last set drop set, 6 sets of calves			
	Flat flyes 27kg 2 sets, cable cross overs 2 sets to fail			
	Amino load	150		80
12:30	chicken, 1 cup lemon tea with ½ lemon in it	180	30	
	Spud	150		30
	After workout had some photos done by Bob. Happy, went home with Jon posing very hard, sunbed 20 minutes. Cooked food for tomorrow			
15:00	Chicken, 1 small coffee	180	30	
	Spud	150		30
16:00	2 creatine			
17:00	Fish, 1 small lemon tea ½ lemon	170	37	
	Veg	80		5
20:00	Tuna, 1 small coffee	100	20	
	Veg	80		5
21:45	Walk 20 mins, 3 times routine			
23:00	Fish	170	37	
	Chicken	180	30	
		2243	235	240

Look very tight sides coming in more and more each day last workout today

Tan on in morning

Just do 2 times round each poses from tomorrow now and let the fullness and sharpness come in. Done all the hard work now just tick

8 glutamine before bed

*Used lemon as a natural diuretic

Thursday 19 October 1995

		Cals	Pro	Carbs
06:15	Up, Sunbed 20 minutes bath and shave and good scrub			
	Eggs, small coffee	90	30	
	Put first coat tan on went on very well look very sharp, striations coming in backside, sides very tight also, very very happy			
08:30	Oat cakes, 1 large coffee Atlanta mug	563	21	91
	Before 10:00 had Amino load and creatine, 2 spoons	150		80
11:00	Chicken, 1 small lemon tea, ½ lemon	180	30	
	*Worked on routine and diet for my off season building, happy with it			
14:15	Chicken, 1 small coffee, ½ Atlanta mug	180	30	
	Spud, 2 creatine	200		30
17:30	Fish, 1 small lemon tea, half lemon	170	37	
	Veg	80		5
19:30	Tuna, 1 small coffee	100	20	
	Veg	80		5
22:45	Fish, 1 small herbal tea	170	37	
	Chicken	180	30	
		2143	235	211

Tan on and 2 times posing tonight, look very sharp legs still holding a little water. Must put feet up and rest Saturday maybe 1 – hour or so tomorrow as well

Keep everything the same – don't alter

8 glutamine before bed

*Something I did then and always do now. As soon as a goal is just within reach, I start to plan another. This does two things for me; one, it takes away the stress of the show/goal as you are reframing it and looking past it. This then stops the anxiety building for the show which stops the adrenalin blowing up, which would do you no good for condition. So I used to plan out a routine, read about things to do in the off season – maybe plan a powerlifting meet, just something to reframe. And two, is it keeps you calm – focused but not so focused that it bubbles up and overspills. This would be no good at all. I called it reframing as in reframing my mind to another goal.

Friday 20 October 1995, still 1.5 litres of water. Two days to go

		Cals	Pro	Carbs
06:15	Up sunbed 20 minutes, shower shave and tan on			
	Eggs, 1 small coffee	90	30	
08:45	Oat cakes 1 large coffee	563	21	90
	*Look very tight again this morning legs look tighter as well, bum coming through also			
	Up to ¼ to 11 had amino load and creatine	150		80
11:00	Chicken, 1 small lemon tea and lemon in	180	30	
	Spud	150		30
13:00	Went home sorted my bag out for Sunday			
14:00	Chicken, 1 small coffee	180	30	
	Spud	150		30
16:00	2 spoons creatine			
17:00	Fish, 1 small lemon tea ½ lemon	170	37	
19:30	Tuna, 1 small coffee	100	20	
	Veg	80		5
	Last big clean round in gym thank god, knackered			
	Home 2 times posing and tan on			
23:00	Fish	170	37	
	Chicken	180	30	
		2163	235	235

Look very very tight back sharpest ever, and chest best it's ever been still very full even when freezing cold still round

Legs holding slight amount of water due to being on them all day no more posing just rest up tomorrow and get ready for the big battle on Sunday

8 glutamine before bed

*Note – I still kept oat cakes in and Amino Load even though no workouts now. This was again just keeping things the same. If I had have cut them out like many would do, in a bit of a panic, then I would have flattened out. Doing this "the same" made me full to bursting – without an overspill. There was no overspill because I was eating "normal" no extra, "normal" only the activity was lower. This allowed a "natural" not a forced fill out and loss of water – so I was full and ripped. Every bodybuilder's dream.

Saturday 21 October 1995, half of 1.5 litre bottle water today

		Cals	Pro	Carbs
05:30	Lemon			
07:00	Up sunbed 20 minutes, look very very tight best ever. Legs sharper this morning must make sure I rest them today let them come out.			
	*Tan very dark so just put a coat of Boots No 7 on this morning, coffee small			
08:00	Eggs, as normal	90	30	
09:00	Oat cakes, 1 normal size coffee	563	21	90
	Packed up food Louise cooked last night, sorted out for tomorrow and made sure we have everything			
	At about 08:30 amino load and creatine	180		80
11:00	Chicken, 1 small lemon tea, ½ lemon	180	30	
	Spud	150		30
	Went to gym did some bits and bobs			
14:00	Home Chicken, 1 small coffee	180	30	
	Spud	150		30
14:45	Set off to Corby, nice stead laid back drive			
17:15	In hotel fish, 1 small lemon tea, ½ lemon	170	37	
	Veg	80		5
	Chilled out in room watching telly put some tan on look very very tight legs look best ever also			
20:00	Tuna, 1 small coffee	100	20	
	Veg	80		5
				240
	From about 20:30 onwards had some wine, ½ a small bottle ½ of 25cl about a large glass			
23:00	Fish, 1 cup coffee small	170	37	
	Chicken	180	30	
		2263	235	

Supplements as normal

5 Amino each meal 1 ½ gram Vit C each meal 1
*Power Cuts up to 20:00 meal

8 glutamine before bed

*Power Cuts were by Tropicana – L-Carnitine, B Vitamins and cider vinegar supplement.

*Tan was Pro-tan. Then the last day I put on Boots No.7 mouse on, this gave the Pro-tan a deep – not a matt look – deeper redder brown that made you stand out on stage. I would use almond oil and baby oil mixed together on top of it before stage.

Almond oil is thicker – baby oil gives you the sheen.

I would mix half and half in a small bottle and put on a light coat on the highlight areas – not all over.

So:

Cap of shoulders

Upper chest

Tense the abs and put on top of them

Upper back

Outer triceps

Tense biceps and put on top of peak

Sweep of quads – tense quads and put oil on outer quad

Tense calves and put on top of calf

Think about how the lights will hit you, this made everything stand out more. Nothing is worse on stage than oil all over someone and it running everywhere and down them. Firstly it looks unprofessional, and secondly you cannot see all of your hard work.

Sunday 22 October, todays the day hopefully the best day in my bodybuilding career

		Cals	Pro	Carbs
05:00	Up electric shave and tan on face and a bit more on legs, first look at myself, very, very tight on legs, striations all over the hamstrings and calves don't look like mine			
	Skin very thin all over and round and full, very happy			
05:30	Oat cakes, small coffee	563	21	90
	2 spoons creatine in the dregs of coffee, read a bit of Platz book again and chilled out			
08:00	More tan on back look very tight even in bad light legs still cannot believe they're mine			
	Chicken, 1 small lemon tea, ½ lemon	180	30	
	Spud	150		30
	Just gone 10:00 now sat at show feet up and very relaxed must keep my head together today is the day I will win			
11:00	Chicken, 1 small water	180	30	
	Spud	150		30
13:30	Tuna, 1 small water	100	20	
	Veg	80		5
15:30	Spud, 1 small water	150		30
	Chicken, 1 creatine	180	30	
	Before night show had loads of chocolate then before going on and it made loads of difference			
	I won in the best nick I have ever been in I am so happy with everything			

Note – as I said this was my seventh attempt at winning this show – I was over the moon.

I can remember being in tears when I won, I know, soft git but that's me. After this show I tried for years to win the Worlds, always back to the drawing board. Always slowly, slowly improving, until I won in 2007. But that's another story.

Autumn 2000

Five years on for Louise and I and a hell of a lot had changed. Ten years in the gym business now and we had expanded taking more floor space in the old mill that housed Future Bodies Gym. We now had and had filled the 10,000 square feet of gym with the best equipment certainly in the UK at the time. We had two and three of each piece and three of each dumbbell up to over 60kg, which was unusual for gyms in those days that were privately owned. Gods truth people used to travel from all over the UK to visit our gym. It was hard work but we were very proud.

Many years later when we sold everything when Louise was ill, we built a very small home gym and worked with only a handful of people, we realised that this was a much better life choice, and balance of work to life was far better – hindsight.

98 saw us blessed with Molly and at this point she was growing fast. It would be another year – 2001, until Louis came along.

99 had seen me win the European Championships and I had got even more into abbreviated routines and HIT style training.

2000 the entries that follow showed the biggest gain in size in my life – this journal I wanted to include as not everyone wants to compete – and this entry shows just pure size and strength building work.

Enjoy.

This will be of most interest to readers as this was the year that I made the best gains of my life.

I had always erred on the side of lower sets and harder work throughout my years of training, I knew of all body HIT programs and had had done them on and off with only a few gains.

I was soon to discover my problem with only a few gains was because of a number of mistakes on my part; 1) I never trained hard enough and 2) I needed to make sure recovery was just as important as the workout itself. Following is the account of the wake-up call that was HIT training.

The Day HIT Training – Hit Me – Literally

Looking in my journal, Thursday 1 September 2000. I can remember the day like it was yesterday. It was a nice, end of the summer evening as my training partners, Rob and Chris, pulled down a back street in Barnsley, England. We were looking for a small gym that a buddy of mine had been training in for 12 or so weeks, when he turned up for a workout at my place, Future Bodies in Morley, Leeds at the time – I could not believe the gains he had made. He told me about a couple in Barnsley that had trained him H.I.T (high intensity training) style. One phone call and days later, there we were.

As I understood, it was very small, and down behind a row of tenement houses. All we could see was rows of garages, nothing anywhere to indicate a gym. Then I noted one of the dilapidated garages had one of its black wooden double doors open a little, my first thought was to see if anyone was in there, so I got out of the car and headed towards it. As I got closer I could see the familiar steel box section that everyone that loves weights can spot a mile off, as a bench or rack.

I waved the lads to get out of the car and we made our way to a small double garage. Inside we found some heavy steel homemade equipment spread around the outside of a huge hole in the middle of the floor. Everything looked homemade and heavy, apart from an old Nautilus Leg Extension sort of perched right over the hole. Little did we know we were in HELL. Mick and Sue Moran greeted us 'in hell'. A couple, in their 50's, Mick a thick set guy, kind of tough looking and Sue a quiet spoken women that betrayed how evil a streak run through her. My buddies and I chatted a little with them and Mick asked who would be going first. I said I would, looking all-full of myself. I had been working the HIT trail for a while now but on a split routine. I figured how hard could this be? I had not directly said this to Mick but on the phone expressed that I trained HARD and had done some shows!! Yada yada yada. So in his mind, he was out for blood, as he knew I did not 'TRAIN HARD'. He said, "Just do as you are told – exactly as I tell you". "Yes sir" I said, by now my heart had sunk into my ass.

From the pages of my Journal

Not that I need reminding that much – god the workout is seared into my soul. It goes down as one of my all-time hardest workouts. Why? Well for one it was a hell of a shock; I had never trained that hard before. It took all I had to keep going – pride, balls, stubbornness. Whatever it was – I had to find it.

From that day on I had a high water mark to reach for. Here is the workout.

Squat – 30kg a side, slow and deep descending I would say for I guess 5 to 7 seconds negative (lowering), then a pause at the bottom for a second, then up. This was for 20 reps. Frigging hell I thought after these what the hell have I let myself in for? No rest.

Leg Extension – full range of movement, pause at the top, weights lightly clicked behind. I found myself feeling for the click, it seemed a world away – CLICK – and up, no kick, squeeze at the top. They were both in each ear – 20 reps, get 20 reps! I was in a world of pain. Every time I failed they dropped the weight "keep going – you're not done 20 reps". How the hell I got them I do not know, I was out of it. Here's the point I let out a "what the f" as I got off the Leg Extension and they put me – 'put me' under the Squat.

Squat – yes I kid you not, same weight same style – forced reps the works till 20, this was torture I thought I going to fall flat out. I don't know how but I did them, it seemed endless. The bastards. No rest at all, I was pushed over to a dip and chin homemade box steel unit in the corner.

Chins – at last something I can do well I thought. Nope – not happening, again not the way I had done them. They had me take an underhand grip – pause at the stretch and pause at the top – the very top. This was for 12 reps, arms and back screaming, made me forget my legs for a spell. Till I stepped off the frame and nearly fell in the hole. Again they moved me with no rest on to a Decline Bench. As they then lifted the bar off the Squat stands and passed it too me, 30kg a side.

Decline Press – for chest, they had me push down towards my groin and squeeze my chest hard, forced reps to 12.

Oh my god what the hell is this I thought, my whole body is shot to bits! I rolled (fell) off the bench and as instructed sat on the floor and was handed a small bar on a Low Pulley Row.

Low Pulley Row – it was heavy "come on strong little man" Mick said as after 6 or so reps he was giving me forced reps to reach 12. Each rep the stretch was held and at the contraction. Sue kept you in the right alignment and was just pure frigging evil – hold – hold – hold – chest up squeeze. I wanted to punch them both but I could not have fought my way out of a paper bag at this point, instead I just screamed and got my 12.

They then made me sit straddled across the Decline Bench and handed me the bar for a Behind Neck Press.

Behind Neck Press – no idea what was on the bar, I could not see or even think at this point. Every rep was like a max rep, held in the bottom and top, stretch and squeeze. Bloody agony! I was shaking so much everything on me was switching off, I got 12 with I think some help, or lots of it.

The bar was whipped off me and then again pushed into the corner, I felt like I was going to explode I was in so much pain and so pumped.

Dips – on the frame, "deep – deep – stretch – hold – then tense at the top", bellowed at each side of me. I got 12; they would not let me get off till I did. These were done in a Rest Pause Style.

I stepped off the frame "nearly there" said Mick as he handed me the bar again.

Curls – I could hardly hold the bar, my arms felt like sponge, it was the hardest set of curls ever, then or since – 12. That frigging 12 again.

Again I was pushed over to the Low Pulley area that also was a Push down with a rope. These did not register at all, 12 with most of them being forced reps.

Dips. I kid you not, I almost cried here. I did 3 reps; I could not for my life do another rep. Mick made me do 9 negatives – stepped up and lowered myself to the bottom, slow. I was screaming like a pig. Done! Said Mick, I dropped to the floor like a stone. The cold mucky cold concrete floor felt like the best thing in the world, I wanted it to soak me up I was in so much pain – everywhere; my whole body was in shock. I moaned like a baby and looked over at the lads, their faces froze in horror. I felt the wave build – I am going to be sick! It scrambled outside, stumbled on a patch of grass outside, fell on my knees and let it rip. It was like a possession of sorts – projectile was not the word. I thought it would never stop, when it did I rolled on the back street between the garages and soaked up as much cold concrete floor as I could.

I lay there for a long time, enough for me to smile as Chris made his way to the sick patch of grass. I smiled at him and gave him the thumbs up. Not long after Rob joined in the laying down in the street party, it took us a while to get up and head home. When we had overcome the shock we chatted about what had just happened.

I voiced that I thought we trained hard and clearly we did not. All of us vowed to train hard as possible and make some gains.

The Gain

For the next twelve weeks I trained harder than I had done up to that point in any of my training life. My weight was 157 or so and I was fair lean at the start of the HIT program we set upon. In 12 weeks I gained like never before topping at 175 and only a slight difference in in leanness. At 5.3 I looked like a box and was strong as a bull.

Here is the base program:

• Squats

• Leg Extensions

• Chins

• Decline Press

• Deadlift

• Shoulder Press

• Curls Thick Bar

• Rope Pushdown

• Dips

• Calf Raise

One set each to fail, aiming for 12 reps.

When I got 12 the weight went up. Simple, just killed it every time.

Why did I stop? After more than two years of training the HIT way I was getting to the point of being scared to train. Yes you read that right – scared. The workouts were that brutal I was hating my training. The gains had been awesome but the romance had faded, so I used other forms of working out and although productive, nothing was or ever has been as productive as the HIT program. Why HIT now? Well as the years have gone on, I have trained hard – not balls to the wall – but hard. I can tolerate it now, training very hard is a learned skill and I have had a lot of years of practice of touching the edge. In order to make gains there has to be a trigger, and intensity is the best way to trigger growth.

A little discussion here on training hard as many out there will not get this concept. Yes there are gyms full of guys who never seem to do a great deal other than mess about with their phone between sets. Well unless you are from Mars you must understand that many – many – of these kids are not let's say, unassisted.

The normal guys, with normal hormones and recovery need to work with Mother Nature not against her. To grow, and for body composition to alter for the better, more muscle less fat – there HAS TO BE a stimulus, a trigger.

This has to come in the form of a bloody hard workout. If you do what your body is capable of, you will not change. Read that again – you will not change. Now the laws of nature state that if you train hard you cannot train long. You cannot sprint a mile, so the harder you push the workout, the less you can tolerate in volume. Simply put here, if you want to grow and be more muscular and leaner – kick the crap out of yourself on a few hard basic exercises, get out of the gym, eat good food and wait till you feel recovered. Then kick the crap out of yourself again. Honest to god it boils down to something as simple as this.

As you will see from the entries here I trained every 4th to 5th day and started adding calories up from all food sources. I eventually at around the 12 weeks mark topped out at 12 stone 7 and with the same bodyfat percentage. I looked huge at that weight, a little fluffy, but not fat by any means.

To this day if a person wants to gain good size and strength I will advocate this type of program.

I often return to something very similar, every year or so to keep me honest and to enjoy the thrill of hard work.

I always, always lean up first, it burns that many calories I then feel starving all the time, a sure sign that the growth mechanism has been triggered.

Enjoy the pages ahead, train hard and make sure you rest and recover.

Thursday 21 September 2000

06:45	Up, cereal	600	30	70
	Protein	100	25	
11:00	Tuna and cottage cheese	190	42	
	Spud	200		40
15:00	Tuna and cottage cheese	190	42	
	Spud	200		40
18:00	Myoplex by EAS	260	42	25
	Toast	200		40
09:30	Workout			

At a placed just out of Barnsley, a chap called Mick and his wife Sue did all over body. Hardest workout ever.

Squats about 20 and 10kg, 20 reps slow and strict

Leg extension 20 reps dropping as needed then squats again 20 reps then chins underhand slow and strict, 12 reps then decline press 45 degree 20kg and 10kg x 12

Then low pully rows 12 reps then shoulder press 12 reps then dips 12 reps, then curls 12 reps then rope pushdowns 12 reps. Then dip again with negs

Sick as a dog after that

20:30	Carb drink	750		200
22:30	Oats and milk and pro	625	48	106
	Needed the carbs			
	Horlicks at bed	200	10	26
		3515	197	547

Friday 22 September 2000

All week around 4000 calories on hols

Tuesday 26 September 2000

All-over body workout, no thighs killed from last Thursday most they have ever hurt in 20 years

Saturday 30 September, on way home 6 hour delay

06:45	Up eggs	180	12	
08:00	Toast	400	12	80
	Cereal	350	10	30
12:00	Cheese sarnie	600	25	50
	Nytro Pro 40	125	20	15
15:00	Cheese sarnie	600	25	50
	Nytro Pro 4	250	40	30
07:00	On plane			
	Chicken	100	15	
	Veg and spud	150		25
	Pud	200		35
19:00	Pro	100	25	
20:30	Eggs	360	18	
	Toast	200	6	40
	Horlicks at bed	200	10	26
	In day just fruit	100		
	Aim is 3800 calories	3915	198	381

Sunday 1 October 2000

07:30	Up			
08:30	Oats	360	11	90
	Milk	180	8	16
	Raisins	70		20
11:00	Nytro	250	40	30
	10 dates	228		60
	Workout – squats 20kg + 10kg, 20			
	Leg extension black one 30kg, 5			
	Under chins 10kg, 9			
	Decline press 20kg + 15kg, 9			
	Deadlifts 2.5 plates rack, 10			
	Shoulder press machine new one 15kg on bottom pin, 10			
	Curls thick bar, 7			
	Rope push 8 plates, 7			
	Dips, 6			
	Calf raise 15 plates, 12			
14:00	No forced reps or negs			
	Pro, 10 spoons maltodextrin creatine and whey and vitamins	500	25	100
16:30	Muesli	300	10	60
	Half Nytro	125	20	15
19:00	Eggs	360	18	
	Cheese	120	7	14
	Toast	300	9	60
20:30	Rice pud	150	10	25
	Banana	100		20
21:30	Weetabix and milk	550	12	50
	Half Nytro	125	20	15
		3718	172	575
		Too low		

Monday 2 October 2000

06:15	Up ache from yesterday			
07:30	Oats	360	11	90
	Milk	100	6	12
	10:30 Cheese sarnies	620	26	100
12:30	Muesli	360	10	60
	Nytro half	125	20	15
	Apple	60		15
16:00	Bagel	240	11	40
	Nytro	250	40	30
19:00	Yogurts	300	14	30
	Nuts	250	20	25
10:00	Eggs	360	18	
	Toast	400	12	80
	Horlicks	200	10	26
	Cheese in egg	120		
		3745	198	523

Still low must get up there

Tuesday 3 October 2000

06:15	Up			
07:00	Oats	360	11	90
	Goats milk	180	8	16
10:30	Beef sarnie in bagel	450	31	40
	Banana	100		20
	Apple	60		15
13:00	Beef sarnie in bagel	450	31	40
	Dates	228		60
17:30	Muesli	360	10	60
	Nytro	125	20	15
19:00	Nuts	250	20	25
19:30	Yogurt	150	7	14
22:00	Cheese	240	14	30
	Toast	400	12	80
	Toast	200	6	40
	Peanut butter	100	4	
		3653	174	545

Wednesday 4 October 2000

06:45	Up			
08:00	Oats	360	11	90
	Milk	180	8	16
	Raisins	70		20
09:00	Raisins	70		20
11:00	Chicken	180	30	
	Spud	200		40
13:30	Muesli	430	10	60
	Cottage	200	26	10
17:00	Bagel	240	11	40
	Nytro	250	40	30
	Fruit in day	160		35

19:30	Nytro	250	40	30
	Banana	100		20
	Eggs	360	18	
	Cheese	120	7	14
	Toast	400	12	80
	Horlicks	200	10	26
		3770	225	531

Thursday 5 October 2000

06:15	Up			
	Carb drink	200		50
	(* improvement)			
	Squats 20kg plus 10kg plus 1 ¼ kg x 18*			
	Leg extension 30kg x 5			
	Underhand chins 10kg plus bar 9* (because of bar)			
	Decline press 20kg + 5kg x 10*			
	Shrugs 100kg x 9.5			
	Shoulder press machine 15kg 11.5*			
	Curl machine 4 plates x 6 ½			
	Pushdowns 8 plates x 7			
	Dips 7*			
	Calf raise 16p x 11*			
09:00	Carbo and pro and creatine	525	20	115
12:00	Muesli 6oz	640	15	80
	Banana	100		20
16:00	Tuna	200	40	
	Spud	200		40
19:00	Bagel	240	11	40
	Pro and a little milk	200	30	10
22:00	Eggs	360	18	
	Toast	400	12	80
	Horlicks at bed	200	10	26
	In day ½ flap jack	250	3	25
	Apple	60		15
		3575	159	501

Friday 6 October 2000, just cals as I am eating 60 – 25 – 15

06:30	Up	
07:30	Shredded wheat	240
	Milk	180
11:00	Tuna	200
	Soup in both	75
	Spud	200
14:00	Bread and tuna	200
17:00	Pro	250
	Bagel	240
	Scone	300
20:00	Nytro	250
	In day fruit	160
	Raisins	70
	½ flap jack	250
22:00	Eggs	360
	Toast	400
	Cheese	120
	Horlicks	200
		3695

Saturday 7 October 2000, cheat day

07:30	Up	
09:10	Breakfast at little chef	900
13:00	Nytro	250
	Date and walnut bread	500
16:00	Sarnie at Dave's house Ethan's birthday	650
17:00	Pitta	400
	Spud	200
22:00	Eggs	360
	Toast	400
	Horlicks at bed	200
	Chocolates	500
		4360

Plenty of water, look a little flat at present maybe cals are a little low. Was 11 stone 8lb last week

Weight this week at 19:00 at night this is my time from now on 11 stone 6

Up cals to 4000 a day and plenty of water

Sunday 8 October 2000

Time	Item	Cals
07:30	Up	
08:30	Cereal	600
	Milk	180
11:30	½ Nytro	125
	Carbo	200
	Nuts	200
	Dates	228
14:30	Beef	400
	Spuds	200
	Veg	50
	Yogurt and fruit	250
17:30	Beef	400
	Spuds	200
	Veg	50
	Gravy on beef	100
20:00	Nuts and dates	228
		250
22:00	2 eggs	180
	Bagel	240
	Horlicks at bed	4082

Monday 9 October 2000

Time	Item	Cal
06:30	Up	
07:30	Cereal	600
	Milk	180
11:00	Cheese sarnie	380
	Pro	250
13:00	Cheese sarnie	380
	Pro	250
15:00	Nuts	250
	Dates	228
17:00	Apple and banana	160
18:00	Workout	

* improved, ✗ not, ✓ same

Squats 2 x 20kg + 7.5 x 8*

Leg extensions 30kg x 7*

Underhand chins 10kg plus bar x 9.5*

Decline press 20kg plus 5kg x 9*

Deadlifts 2 ½ plates + 2kg x 9*

Machine shoulder press 17.5kg x 8*

Curls thick x 6✗

Pushdowns 8 plates x 8*

Dips x 7✓

Calves 16 plates x 11✓

Time	Item	Cal
19:00	Pro mix	525
22:00	Shepherd's pie	400
	Yogurt	250
	Horlicks	200
		4113

Tuesday 10 October 2000

06:30	Up	
	Cereal	600
	Milk	180
11:00	Tuna sarnie in bagel	350
	Pro	250
13:00	Muesli	360
	Pro	250
	Apple	60
15:00	Nuts	250
	Dates	228
16:30	Cheese	240
	Bagel	240
19:00	Bagel	240
	Pro ½	125
22:00	Homemade rice pud	600
	Horlicks at bed	200
		4173

Wednesday 11 October 2000

06:45	Up, bath	
07:30	Toast	400
	Pro	200
11:00	Chicken	200
	Spud	200
	Soup	50
14:00	Chicken	200
	Spud	200
	Soup	50
17:00	Pro	250
	Bagel	240
19:30	Nuts and dates	360
	Flap jack	200
	Chicken spuds and pasta	600
	Cereal and Horlicks	550
		3900

Thursday 12 October 2000

06:45	Up	
07:30	Cereal	600
	Milk	180
10:00	Tuna	200
	Rice	400
	Pineapple	200
13:00	Cheese sarnie	600
	Fruit	260
19:00	Pasta bake	450
22:00	Eggs	360
	Toast	400
	Horlicks	200
	Bagel	240
		4090

Friday 13 October 2000

06:00	Up	
	Banana	100
	Raisins	70
07:30	Workout at Nautilus in Pontefract	

Very very good workouts all of us

Leg ext 50kg, 12, leg press one leg alternate 310lb x 6 each, underhand chins 15kg x 8

Pec deck 120lb x 7, decline press machine 11, row machine 150kg x 8.5

Missed out shoulder press weight and reps

Curls 35kg x 7

Pushdowns 100lb x 11, dip x 4

Calf machine 150lb x 9

Abs after 15 minutes 70lb x 11

	OJ drink	300
09:30	Breakfast cereal milk and banana	900
13:00	Tuna bake	400
	Pro	250
16:00	Tuna bake	400
19:00	Bagel	240

Pro	250
Fruit	160
Eggs	360
Toast	400
Horlicks	200
	4030

Note – I had a little dip in calories a couple of week back when I got up over 4000 that's when things really start to happen. Note also – from week one – how strength is steadily increasing when you compare weights from then to further on in this journal you will see that they increased dramatically.

For instance – squats had a 20kg and a 10kg a side, weeks later 2 plates and a 10kg and a 2½ a side. This is what dramatically changed me – and this is the same percentage wise throughout all the exercises.

Saturday 14 October 2000, 11 stone 9

08:30	Up	
09:30	All organic – Bran	200
	Beans	120
	Juice	100
	Toast	100
	Eggs	360
	Cheese	120
	Bagel	240
	Marmalade	100
13:00	Pro	250
	Banana	100
	16:00	Meal out
	Spuds things	450
	Steak	400
	Chips	400
	Pudding	500
	Sweets	500
	Pro at bed	200
		4140

A gain of 3lb it is working, no difference in condition

Sunday 15 October 2000

07:30	Up, bath	
08:30	Cereal*	600
	Milk	180
11:30	Pro	450
	Banana	100
14:30	Tuna sarnie	500
	Nytro	250
17:30	Beef	450
	Spud	250
	Veg	50
20:30	Spud	200
	Half organic Pizza home made	500
	Yogurt	300
	½ Carbo in day	200
		4030

*Point – when I say cereal I did a mix of muesli, shredded wheat, and oats mixed together

Monday 16 October 2000

06:45	Up	
	Breakfast, cereal	600
	Milk	180
	In day at collage	
	Sarnie bread	450
	Cheese	580
	Chutney	100
	Banana	100
	Apple	60
	Pro	250
16:30	Mince	300
	Pitta	130
19:30	Pro	250
	Bagel	240
22:00	Rice pud	500
	Horlicks at bed	200
		3960

Tuesday 17 October 2000

Time	Item	Value
06:45	Up	
	Cereal	480
	Milk	180
	In day at collage	
	Muesli	450
	Pros	500
	Bananas	200
	Apple	60
	Bagel	240
16:30	Bagel	240
	Cheese	240
18:00	Workout	
	Squats 2 x 20kg + 7.5, 10*	
	Leg extensions 30kg, 8*	
	Underhand chins 15kg, 5*	
	Pec deck 8 plates 8*	
	Press machine decline 7 plates x 5	
	Deadlifts 2.5 plates + 2.5 x 9 ✓	
	Shoulder press 17kg x 10*	
	Curls machine 4 plates x 8*	
	Dips x 7 ✓	
	Calves 17 plates 9.5*	
19:00	Pro	355
	Carbs	400
22:00	Rice pud homemade again	500
	Horlicks at bed	200
		4045

This bar was a Buffalo Bar – a little heavier and curved
Note also I am squatting to pins

Wednesday 18 October 2000

In day	480
Cereal	180
Chicken	180
Spud	200
Chicken	180
Spud	200
Fruit	260
Tuna	100
Cottage	150
Pro	250
Pro	250
Bagel	240
Dates	200
Supper eggs	360
Toast	400
Yogurt	300
Horlicks at bed	200
	4130

Thursday 19 October 2000

06:45	Up	
	Breakfast cereal	450
	Milk	180
	In day	
	Cheese	240
	Bagel	240
	Muesli	450
	Cottage	300
	Bananas	200
	Apple	60
	Pros	500
	Pasta and chicken and cheese	500
	Pro	355
	Toast	400
		3875

*Point – very busy at this point so just listed foods
for day, in no order

Friday 20 October 2000, 11 stone 9 at night look leaner than last week, muscle is going on need to up calories more, 4300 from now on

In day	
Cereal	380
Milk	180
Chicken and pasta	400
Pro	250
Chicken and pasta	400
Pro	250
Fruit	260
Regen	355
Bagel	240
Pro	250
Rice pud home made	500
Horlicks at bed	200
Wine	70

A few raisins yogurt coated	200
Some yogurt	300
	4235

*Point – Regen was a meal replacement product I produced, at this point I was testing these, eventually I sold them in the gym

Saturday 21 October 2000

07:30	Up	
09:00	Breakfast out about	900
11:30	Yogurt	300
	Banana	100
	Workout	
	Leg extensions 50kg x 10*	
	Leg press 6 plates a side x 6*	
	Under arm chins 17.5 x 6.5*	
	Press decline 20kg + 5kg + 2.5kg x 7*	
	Shrugs 100kg x 9*	
	Shoulder press 20kg x 8*	
	Curls thick x 7*	
	Pushdowns 8 plates x 5*	
	Dips x 7✓	
	Calves 17 plates x 22*	
13:00	Pro regen and carbs	755
15:30	Eggs	360
	Toast	400
18:00	Fish and chips	700
	Ice cream	210
	Sweets	400
	Cereal	600
		4725

Weight 11 stone 10, after 3 poos and training, and sunbed (sweating) feel and look leaner but a lot bigger

Sunday 22 October 2000

Ate well at Bridlington all day, 4300 calories

Monday 23 October 2000

06:30	Up hardly any sleep	
	Oat cakes	450
	Milk	180
11:00	Tuna sarnie	540
	Milk	180
13:00	Tuna sarnie	540
	Fruit	260
16:00	Eggs	360
	Cheese	120
	Bagel	240
17:00	Muesli	460
	Pro	250
22:00	Rice pud home made	500
	Horlicks at bed	200
		4280

Tuesday 24 October 2000, 11 stone 10 big and full still same condition its working

Food today birthday 4300 calories

Wednesday 25 October 2000

	Oats	380
	Milk	180
10:00	Chicken	200
	Spud	200
13:30	Muesli	450
16:30	Pro	200
	Banana	100
	Apple	60
	Cottage	300
19:00	Bagel	240
	Pro	355
22:00	Eggs	360
	Toast	400

Dates	185
Nuts	300
Horlicks at bed	200
	4110

A bit low today

Thursday 26 October 2000

05:50	Up	
	Banana	100
	Dates	185
07:00	Workout at Pontefract	
	Leg extensions 55kg x 13lb	
	Leg press 1 leg 310lb 8 each	
	Chins 17.5 x 8	
	Peck deck 120lb x 9	
	Decline press 130lb x 9	
	Rows 150lb x 10	
	Press 110lb x 9.5	
	Curls 35kg x 8	
	Pushdowns 110lb x 9	
	Dips 4	
	Calves press 160lb x 10	
09:00	Oats	380
	Brown sugar	60
11:30	Stew about	400
	Bread	400
15:00	Stew about	400
	Bread	400
17:30	Bagel	240
	Pro	250
19:00	Pro	250
21:00	Yogurt	300
22:00	Eggs	360
	Bagel	240
	Pro at bed	200
		4165

Friday 27 October 2000

Calories 4300

Saturday 28 October 2000, 11 stone 10

See what weigh later after more water
Lost a bit I think it is water balance

	Breakfast organic Weetabix	280
	Milk	180
12:30	Steak	400
	Spud	200
15:00	Egg sarnie	400
	Bars organic	260
17:30	Eggs	360
	Bagel	210
19:30	Meal out	
	Prawn	250
	Steak	600
	Sauce	200
	Pud	400
	Pro	200
	Banana	100
		4040

Very underestimated a bit there

Sunday 29 October 2000

	In day	
	Weetabix	280
	Milk	180
	Carbo	400
	Spud	200
	Cottage	150
	Pro	150
	Pizza out with Dad and Janet	1000
18:30	Eggs	360
	Bagel	240
	Pro	250
	Sweets	400
	Regen at bed	355
	Banana	100
		4065

Monday 30 October 2000

Food in day 4375 wrote down all foods on a card and totted up calories

Workout

Squats 2 plates plus 10kg x 8*

Leg extensions 30kg x 10*

Chins 20kg, 7.5*

Decline 20kg + 7.5 + 1 ¼, x 8*

Deadlifts 3 plates x 8*

Press 20kg + 1 ¼ x 8*

Curls machine 4 plates + 2 ½ x 8*

Pushdowns 8 plates x 11*

Dips x 6✗

Toe press 100kg x 17✓

Trap bar deadlifts

Tuesday 31 October 2000

	Cereal and milk	460
13:00	Beef	400
	Spud	200
	Beans	120
14:30	Pros	500
	Banana	100
16:30	Turkey mince	
	Beef sarnie	400
	Spud	200
19:30	Beef	400
	Spud	200
	Nuts	250
22:30	Eggs	360
	Cheese	120
	Toast	400
	Horlicks	200
		4310

Wednesday 1 November 2000

Foods up to coming home	2870
Eggs	360
Toast	400
Yogurt	300
Banana	100
Horlicks	200
	4230

Feel massive at present chest mega full and delts and legs only a slight difference in abs

Thursday 2 November 2000

08:00	Breakfast	460
	Milk	190
	Banana	100
12:00	Beef stew	400
	Bread	400
	Milk	190
	Apple	60
16:00	Beef stew	400
	Bread	400
	Milk	190
17:00	Bagel	240
	Pro	250
21:00	Yogurt	300
	Eggs	360
	Toast	250
		4190

Friday 3 November 2000

Cereal	460
Milk in day 4 pints	270
	270
	270
	270
Tuna	200
Cottage	300
Spuds	600
Bagels	240
Fruit	360
Eggs	360
Toast	400
Yogurt	300
	4300

Saturday 4 November 2000

06:45	Got out of bed 07:30	
	Breakfast	
	Bacon	160
	Beans	120
	Eggs	360
	Weetabix	230
11:00	Milk semi skim	260
	Bananas	200
12:30	Trained	

✓ same, * up, × down

Leg extension 55kg x 12*

Leg press 6 plates x 9*

Chins 20kg, 4 ¾ (just a little off top)*

Peck deck 8 plates x 9*

Nytram chest press 20kg plus 15kg x 5*

Shrugs 110kg x 9*

Press 20kg + 1 ¼ x 9 + 1 neg*

Curls bar x 7 ✓

Dips x 6 ×

Toe press 130kg x 11*

14:00	Regen	355
	Carbs	400
15:00	Eggs	360
	Toast	400
17:00	Milk (skim)	190
18:30	Steak	500
	Spuds	300
	Veg	50
	Sweets cheat	500
		4435

Sunday 5 November 2000

All foods I list are organic

Eaten today

Eggs	360
Bagel	240
Cheese	120
Spud	200
Milk in day skimmed	190
½ milk	90
Flap jack	400
Tuna	200
Spud	250
Chicken	200
Spud	250
Carrot cake	300
Beef sarnie	250
Yogurt	300
Nuts	
Dates	528
Yogurt	300
	4368

Monday 6 November 2000

Up to supper	3565
Tuna sarnie	367
Bagel	240
Horlicks at bed	200
	4372

Look big and full

If not any heavier at this week's weigh in will up to 4500 – as my base

Tuesday 7 November 2000

In day

Cereal	600
Milk	190
Milk	190
Fruit	160
Cheese and bagel sarnies	240
	480
Butter	100
Milk	190
Bar	300
Chicken	200
Rice	200
Eggs	360
Toast	400
Horlicks	200
	*528
	4338

*Nuts and dates forgot them

Wednesday 8 November 2000, 11 stone 12.5 pounds

3100 up to supper

When in yogurt	300
Eggs	360
Toast	400
Horlicks at bed	200
	4360

Thursday 9 November 2000

2 bananas (came back up no count)

Pro after workout	755
Breakfast crunch	430
Milk	180

Workout

Squats 2 plates plus 10kg, buff bar x 9* - buffalo bar, a curved bigger bar

Leg extensions 35kg x 7*

Chins 20kg x 8*

Decline thick 15kg plus 2.5 and 1.25 x 9* - thick bar weighed 47kg, before adding weight on

Deadlifts 3 plates x 9*

Press 20kg + 2 ½ x 7.5*

Curl machine 4 plates + 1 ¼ x 8 ✓

Dips 5 ½ ✗

Toe press 140kg x 9*

Milk in day	1040
Spud	200
Tuna	100
Cottage	150
Bagel	240
Pasta bake	400
Fruit	200
Fish in bread	500
Horlicks	200
	4395

Friday 10 November 2000

Cereal	460
Fruit	260
Milk in day	1040
Pasta bake	400
Bar	400
Spud	200
Tuna	100
Cottage	150
Bagel	240
Quiche	360
Soup	75
Bread	400
Nuts and dates	528
	4613

Felt very hungry today

Saturday 11 November 2000, 11 stone 12

Good day today

Been into town and bought a couple of mags
Batman and Wolverine

Eaten today

Eggs	360	
Cheese	120	
Bagel	240	
Milk in day	270	
	270	
	270	
Bun	250	
Fruit	260	
Fruit	160	
Yogurt	300	
Pizza	1000	
Chicken	180	lunchtime
Rice	200	
Bar	350	
Nuts	150	
Horlicks at bed	200	
	4580	

Hovering between 11 stone 13 and 12 stone today

Sunday 12 November 2000

Good day again, got most of my homework done also went to see Billy Elliott, very good

Morning cereal	460
Bagel	240
Milk in morning	270
	270
Fruit	160
Bar	350
Chicken thing	300
Spud	250
Veg	50
Milk	270

Eggs	360
Rice	200
Quiche	180
Nuts and raisins yogurt coated at pictures, lolly	800
Yogurt	300
	4460

Monday 13 November 2000

Eaten today

Cereal	600
Beef	350
Bagels	240
	240
Fruit	260
Bar	400
Milk	270
	270
Liver	200
Spud	200
Sauce	50
Regen	355
Milk	270
Rice pud	430
Nuts	150
Fruit	100
	4385

Got a sword from Steve Logan today, awesome just like the Conan one – this he made for me himself.

Tuesday 14 November 2000, 12 stone

Food today up to this point	3380
Turkey and veg	300
Bagel	240
Horlicks at bed	200
	4120

Wednesday 15 November 2000

05:50	Banana	100
	Raisins	40
07:00	Workout Pontefract	
	Leg extension 60kg x 12	
	Leg press 1 leg 335 – 12 each	
	Chins 20kg x 8.5	
	Peck deck 130lb x 8	
	Decline push 140lb x 10	
	Row 160lb x 9	
	Curls 35kg x 9	
	Pushdowns 120lb x 9	
	Dips 4.5	
	Calves 170lb x 10	
	Abs 80lb x 10, drop 60lb x 5 , 40lb x 6	
	Doing well, sick as well but only water came up, felt big	
09:00	Cereal	650
	Milk in day	1080
11:00	Pasta bake	400
	Scone wholemeal	300
16:00	Pasta bake	400
19:00	Regen	355
	Fruit	60
	½ Louise organic bake	700
	Horlicks at bed	200
		4285

Thursday 16 November 2000

06:30	Up	
	Eaten today	
	Cereal	460
	Date thing	700
	Cheese bake and tuna	400
	Milk	1080
	Fruit	200

Yogurt	300
Bagel	240
Chicken	200
Spud	200
Pro	250
Banana	100
	4130

Too low, up to 4500 tomorrow

Sat about a lot today so conserved cals, read a lot and played with Molly at night, a bit of drawing for Twiggy, my mate

Trained 5 people

Friday 17 November 2000, 11 stone 12

I think I will hold 12 stone then tighten up and drop a bit as I feel the more muscle I build the more calories I burn

Look big very big for me still see abs and hamstring

Look full try to get above 12 stone over the next few days

Oats	340
Milk	180
Milk in day	1080
Spud	200
Chicken	200
Bagels	240
	240
Eggs	360
Nuts	400
Regen	355
Fruit	300
Toast	400
Cheese	120
	4415

Saturday 18 November 2000

After sunbed today had a check out at gym look very good big, perhaps biggest I have ever looked look lean as well

Eaten today

Eggs	360
Pancakes	300
Banana	100
Cereal	190
Milk	100
Milk in a day	270
	270
Regen	355
Cheese	120
Bagel	240

Meal out celebrating Chris and Gayle having a baby on the way 9 weeks gone

Steak	400
Chips	300
Soup	120
Pudding	450
Bread	200
Yogurt	300
Wine	70
Raisins and nuts	250
	4395

Sunday 19 November 2000

07:30	Up	
	Cereal	190
	Milk	100
	Bagel	240
	Banana	100
	Bagel	240
	Regen	355
12:30	Workout	

Squats 2 plates + 10kg plus 1 ¼, x 9*

Leg extension 35kg x 8.5*

Chins 20kg x 8, 1 forced✗

Decline press, 20kg x 8 (static hold)

Shrugs 110kg x 10*

Press 20kg x 2 ½ x 9

Curl machine 4 plates plus 2 ½ x 8✓

Pushdowns 9 plates x 9*

Dips x 5, 3 negs

Toe press 140kg x 15*

	*Regen	355
	Carb	400
15:00	Meal chicken	300
	Spud	200
	Butter	100
	Veg	20
	Milk in day	270
		270
06:30	Eggs	360
	Toast	400
	Yogurt	400
	Wine	70
		4370

*Note on workouts, I get the carbs in a drink along with protein right after the session.

Monday 20 November 2000

Eat well all day

	3410
Bar	300
Rice pud	430
Horlicks	200
	4340

Tuesday 21 November 2000

Eaten today

Cereal	460
Fruit	180
Milk	270
	270
Cheese	360
Bagels	240
	240
Mince beef	400
Spud	200
Pro mix at gym with carb	400
Regen	355
Banana	100
Milk	270
Later ½ milk	135
Eggs	360
Bagel	240
	4480

Wednesday 22 November 2000

Up to coming in	3995
Bagel	240
Horlicks	200
	4435

Thursday 23 November 2000

Eaten today

Cereal	460
Milk	270
	270
Full fat	360
Bagel	240
Fruit	260
Chicken	400

Spuds	400	
Soup	50	
Eggs	360	
Toast	400	
Yogurt	300	
Nuts and dates in day	528	
Banana	100	
Horlicks	200	
	4598	

Friday 24 November 2000

06:00	Carbo	400
07:30	Workout legs last this workout*	
	Calves standing 18 plates x 12*	
	Peck deck 9 plates x 10*	
	Press Nytram 20kg plus 15kg, x 8* - Nytram was a Hammer type chest press	
	Chins 20kg x 8×	
	Deadlifts 3 plates + 2 ½ x 8*	
	Shoulder press 20kg plus 1 ½ x 11*	
	Curl thick 7 ½ *	
	Dips 6 ½*	
	Squats 2 plates + 10kg + 1 ¼ x 5, drop 10kg plus 1¼ x 6, drop 20kg x 6*	
	Carb and regen	355
		400
	Eggs	360
	Spud	200
	Milk in day	270
		270
	Pro	250
	Spud	200
	Tuna	150
	Cottage	150
	Bagel	240
	Pro	250
	Yogurt	200

Banana	100
Pro	230
Toast and peanut butter	230
	4255

Saturday 25 November 2000, 12 stone

Eggs	180
Cereal	300
Bananas	200
Milk in day	270
	270
Regen	355
Quiche	330
Spud	300
Ice cream	215
Pizza only a little bit	300
Bread	350
Coleslaw	250
Eggs	180
Rice pud	430
Banana	100
Rice	70
	4100

Bodyfat test

168lb
Pec 4
Sub 7
Bicep 2
Triceps 4
Kid 18
Supra 7
Ab 10
Quad 3
Calf 3
Total 58
9% bodyfat, 15.6 bodyfat, (152 lean mass)

Sunday 26 November 2000

Oats	380
Milk	180
Banana	100
Regen	355
Banana	100
Pro	250
Turkey	300
Spud	200
Gravy	100
At movies	
Popcorn	300
Yogurt	300
Apple	60
Eggs	360
Cheese	120
Bagel	240
Milk	180
Nuts and dates	528
Beef mince	250
Horlicks	200
	4513

Monday 27 November 2000

Eggs	180
Weetabix	460
	180
Milk	270
	270
	270
Turkey	200
Bagels	240
Fruit	240
Nuts and dates	528
Rice	300

Chicken	200
Regen	355
Carbo	200
Pro	250
Bagel	240
Horlicks	200
	4583

Tuesday 28 November 2000

Pro	200
Eggs	360
Toast	400
Banana	100
Milk in day	270
	270
Rice	200
Chicken	200
Banana	100
Turkey	100
Spud	150
Cheese sarnie	400
Pro	250
Oats	380
Milk	200
Yogurt	300
Bagel	240
	4120

A bit low today

Wednesday 29 November 2000

06:00   Up

Oats and banana

No record came back up after workout

07:30   Leg extensions 60kg, 10 ¼*

Leg press 6 plates + 10kg x 7*

Chins 20kg, x 8 ½*

Decline press 20kg on thick bar x 9, SH as well*

Shrugs 110kg x 10 ✓

Press machine 20kg + 5 ½ x 8 ½ *

Curl machine 4 plates + 2kg × down

Pushdowns 10kg x 4 weight too heavy

Toe press 140kg x 11 × down

Dips x 6

A few down on this only had about 3 hours sleep
Molly has a cold.

Regen and carbo	355
	400
Cereal	440
Milk	150
Milk in day	270
	270
	270
Chicken	440
Rice and pasta salad (about 500)	500
Chicken	200
Spud	200
Gravy	100
Banana	100
Yogurt	300
Cereal	500
	4495

Thursday 30 November 2000

Up to coming home

	3553
Eggs	360
Bagel	240
Yogurt	300
	4453

Friday 1 December 2000, 12 stone 2

Eaten today

Cereal	460
Milk	1080
Pro	500
Bar	300
Spuds	400
Tuna	200
Cottage	200
Bananas	200
Eggs	360
Bagel toast	400
Yogurt	300
	4400

Saturday 2 December 2000

09:00	Cereal	300
	Milk	250
11:00	Pro regen	355
12:00		355
	Carbo	400
	Banana	100
14:30	Turkey mince	300
	Spud	300
	Cheese	120
16:00	Yogurt	300
18:00	Eggs	360
	Bagel	240
	Oats	630
	Bagel	100
	Egg white	30
		4140

Sunday 3 December 2000

Oats	380
Milk	180
Banana	100
Regen	355
Carbo	200
Banana	100

Workout

Squats 2 plates + 10kg + 2 ½ x 9*

Pullovers 50kg

Decline thick bar 20kg + 1 ½ x 9*

Deadlifts in trap 2 plates + 10kg x 10

Press 20kg + 5kg x 9

Close press thick 50kg bar + 10kg a side in rack x 5

Dumbbell curls 17 ½ x 8

Calf raise 20 plates x 12

Regen	355
Carbo	400
Soup	200
Bread	200
Lamb	300
Pub – spud and veg	600
A little ice cream	100
Turkey mince Shepard's Pie and rice	400
Wine	70
Yogurt	300
	4240

Monday 4 December 2000

Up to coming in	3490
Pro	100
Eggs	360
Toast	400
Horlicks	200
	4550

Tuesday 5 December 2000, 12 stone 2 nothing on

Up to coming in	3528
Eggs	360
Toast	400
Horlicks	200
	4488

Wednesday 6 December 2000

Up to coming home	3000
Regen	355
Carbo	400
Eggs	360
Toast	400
	4515

Thursday 7 December 2000

Cereal	460
Milk	180
Milk in day	270
	270
	270
Steak	200
Spud	200
Steak	200
Spud	200
Fruit	260
Pro	250
Bagel	240
Pasta bake	400
Rice pud	500
Milk	100
Yogurt	150
	4150

Friday 8 December 2000

Up to coming home	3495

Includes a pre workout drink

Went to see Mick and Sue in Swinton, did a chest shock

Decline press, peck deck, dips, round this twice then press ups – forced reps on all and negs, then 1 min rest

Then squat 20 reps about 200lb, then leg extensions 20 reps, this was absolute agony

Then chins got 10 then 2 negs, then press behind neck with drop sets, then curls with drop sets

Felt ill but not sick

Eggs	360
Toast	400
Horlicks	200
	4455

Saturday 9 December 2000, 12 stone 1, up calories again 4700 from now

When I get to 12 stone 5 will slow up by adding some aerobics

I think I would be heavier but I am light because of training yesterday

Time	Item	Calories
09:00	Weetabix	240
	Milk	180
10:00	Fruit	160
	Pro	250
12:00	Milk	250
	Milk	250
14:00	Sarnie egg	500
16:00	Pro half MET-Rx	125
	Milk	100
	Bagel	240
18:00	Chicken	200
	Spud	200
	Marg and veg	100
	Rice pud	350
	Banana	100
	Wine	70
	Bar	130
	Yogurt	300
	Rice pud	500
		4245

Sunday 10 December 2000, might up cals today. Feel very big

Chest, triceps and delts kill me today

Time	Item	Calories
	Oats	380
	Milk	180
	Raisins	70
	Pro at gym	355
	Carb	400
	Milk	270
	Apple	60
15:00	Cheese	240
	Toast	400

18:00	Turkey	250
	Turkey gravy	100
	Spud	200
	Yogurt	300
	Fruit	100
	Sweets	330
	Pro	250
		180
	Banana	100
		4165

I have struggled to eat because of a cold I have so I have tried to drink my calories.

*Note of interest – note that I eat nothing special at all just good old basic food. The main base being carbs and keeping the calories up. Plenty of milk, cheese, eggs, fruit, bread, bagels, all high calorie foods. I have said it before and will many times the trigger to change is the hard work – the killer workouts. There has to be a catalyst to it all. Then eat and rest, simple, but hard work is the key to growth.

Monday 22 December 2000

Up to coming in	3845
Eggs	360
Bagel	240
Yogurt	300
	4745

Tuesday 12 December 2000

Up to coming in	3236
Pro	355
Supper rice pud	500
Few dates	150
Yogurt	300
	4541

Wednesday 13 December 2000

Workout

*Hacks 3 plates x 10, drop 2 plates x 4, 1 plate x 6

Pulldowns on Nytram 20kg + 10kg x 9.5

Nytram press 2 plates x 10

Single row 2 plates x 7.5

Press behind neck 15kg x 9

Curls same 6 ¼

Dip 6 ¾

Calf 20 plates x 8

Up to coming home	3610
Eggs	360
Toast	400
	4370

*Note – after a warm up. The program of exercises was done non-stop, only resting was walking from one exercise to the next. Average time was around 15 minutes per workout after 10 or so minutes warming up. I would go, then Rob, then Chris, one person spotting while the other recovers.

Thursday 14 December 2000

Up to coming in	3750
Eggs	360
Bagel	240
Horlicks at bed	200
	4550

Friday 15 December 2000

*Up to coming in	3335
Eggs	360
Bread	300
Yogurt	300
Horlicks	200
	4495

*Up to coming in, was from work - the gym, at about 22:00. I kept my calories noted on a bit of card in my pocket all day.

Sunday 16 December 2000

Eggs	360
Toasted bagel	240
Banana	100
Cheese sarnie	350
Egg sarnie	400
Pro	250
Milk	200
Banana	100
Bagel	240
Chicken	200
Spud	250
Veg and sauce	100
Rice pud	300
Sweets	350
Oats	380
Milk	200
Wine	70
Banana	100
Yogurt at bed	400
	4590

Sunday 17 December 2000

Rice pud	350
Banana	100
Pro and carb	300

Workout

* improve, ✓ same, ✗ down

Squat 2 plates + 10kg + 1 ¼ x 10*

Pullovers 55kg x 8 2 forced*

Decline 20kg + 2 ½ on thick x 9✓

Deadlifts 2 plates + 15kg trap bar x 10*

Press 20kg + 7kg x 9*

Close press 5kg a side on 50kg bar x 5 ✗ bit lighter on weights

Dumbbell curls 17 ½ x 8 ½*

	Calves 21 plates x 9*	
	Regen and carb	355
		400
	Banana	100
	Chocolate nuts at pics, Arnold's new film 6th Day very good	900
18:00	Beef	400
	Spud	200
	Veg and gravy	100
19:00	Yogurt	200
	Bagel	240
	Cheese	120
	Cereal	300
	Yogurt	300
		4365

Monday 18 December 2000

Up to coming in	3735
Eggs	360
Toast	400
Horlicks	200
	4695

Tuesday 19 December 2000, 12 stone 1

Up to coming in	3755
Eggs	360
Toast	400
Horlicks	200
	4715

Wednesday 20 December 2000, 12 stone 2

More water	
Muesli	198
	198
Milk	180

10:00	Regen		355
	Carb		200
11:00	Pasta bake		400
13:00	Pasta bake		400
	Bagel		240
19:00	Regen		355
	Carbo		400
22:00	Rice pud		500
	Pro		250
	Banana		100
			3776

Too low today

Thursday 21 December 2000

Eaten today

Cereal	128
	128
	180
Banana	100
Regen	335
Apple	60
Carbo	200
Spud	200
Chicken	200
Spud	200
Regen	355
Carb	400
Toast	400
Banana	100
Dates	290
Eggs	360
Toast	400
Pro	250
Snack nuts	300
	4586

Friday 22 December 2000

Time	Activity	Value
06:00	Up	
	Banana	100
	Carbo	200
07:30	Workout	

Did this one very slow in style best yet, just all muscle not too sick, killed on legs

NA lift both legs, lower with one negative accentuated

Calves standing 21 plates x 11

Press Nytram 2 plates + 2 ½ x 8

Pulldowns 80kg x 7

Press behind neck 7.5 + 5 x 10

Shrugs 1 plate x 6

Curls 7 ½ + 5kg x 8.5

Pushdowns 10 plates x 7

Dips neg only 20kg x 8

Leg ext NA 30kg x 15 too light

Leg press 100kg x 9

	Carbo and Regen	400
		355
	In day pasta	594
	Turkey mince	500
	Mince pies	500
18:00	Oats	380
	Raisins	70
20:30	Pro	355
	Carbo	200
	Eggs	360
	Bagel	242
	Yogurt	300
		4556

Saturday 23 December 2000

Eaten today

Shredded wheat	210
Milk	180

Banana	100
Regen	355
Carbo	400
Quiche	360
Spud	200
Cheese	120
Christmas cake	400
Chicken	300
Rice	300
Christmas cake	400
Fruit	70
Pro	250
OJ out	350
Cereal	330
Milk	180
	4505

Won £25 at casino

Sunday 24 December 2000

08:30	Up late	
10:00	Oats	380
	Milk	360
	Banana	100
12:00	½ pro	125
	Banana	100
15:00	Chinese	1300
	Christmas cake	400
18:00	Pro	250
	Apple	60
19:00	Toast	300
21:00	Cheese	400
	Biscuits	140
	Wine	70
	Yogurt	300
		4285

A little low but lazy day

Monday 25 December 2000

Christmas day

Tuesday 26 December 2000

Weetabix	128
	128
Milk	180
Banana	100
Meal out	1400
Eggs	360
Bagel	240
Yogurt	300
Christmas cake	600
Bed ½ pro	125
4oz oats	380
	3941

Still low as not doing anything, 12 stone 4

Wednesday 27 December 2000

	Oats	360
	Pro	125
	Banana	100
	Carbo	200
13:00	Workout	

Squats 2 plates + 15kg x 8 fell on 9th*

Pullovers 55kg x 9, slight touch on last one *

Decline 20kg + 2 ½ + 1 1/4 x 7 round *

Deadlifts 3 plates x 10*

Press 20kg x 7 ½ + 1 ¼ x 7 ¼ *

Close press 5kg thick bar x 5 ½ ✓

Dumbbell 17 ½ x 8 ✓

Calves 21 plates x 8 ✗

1 set abs 10kg x 12

Pro	355
Carb	400
Spud	200
Cottage	150
Pro	355
Carb	400
Spud cottage	200
	150
Chicken	200
Spud	200
Cauliflower	150
Bread	200
Wine	70
Cake	400
	4215

Note – decline was always with a thick bar pushing towards the lower body, at finish point the bar was over the belly button, thick bar is/was 47kg, I still have it today.

Thursday 28 December 2000

Ache a lot today doing movements very slow

Oats	360
Pro	125
Raisins	70
Pro	355
Carb	200
Eggs	360
Cheese	240
Bagel	240
Cake	400
Salmon	400
Spuds	300
Yogurt	300
Wine	70
Rice pud	500
	3920

Still low but sat around most of day made a snowman for Molly, fed horses

Friday 29 December 2000

Up to coming in	3050
Chicken	200
Rice	300
Yogurt	300
A bit of cake	300
	4150

Up cals back to 4700 next week

Saturday 30 December 2000

Oats	360
Banana	100
Goats milk	180
Regen	355
Carb	400
Yogurt	300

Banana	100
Milk	300
Chicken	200
Cheese	240
Bread	200
Chocolate	300
	3035

Sunday 31 December 2000

Up to coming home	1557
Bagels	240
	240
Eggs	360
Meal out Claire's	
Soup	400
Salmon	400
Spuds	300
Sauce	200
Pud	500
Yogurt	300
Pro	300
	4797

Feel ever so full after meal at Claire's

Workout did some filming but half way through battery ran out so doing again on Thursday

Calf raise 22 plates x 8, 1F

Press Nytram 2 plates + 2 ½ x 7, 1F

Chin 20kg plate + 1 ½ x 6, 1F

Press behind neck 7 ½ + 5 ½ + 1 ¼ x 7

Shrugs 20kg + 2 ½ x 7

Curls same as PBN x 6

Pushdowns 9 plates x 8

Dips x 3

Leg extensions 40kg x 11 with 1 leg lowering neg

Leg press 120kg x 10 with 1 leg lowering neg

Leg press – negative accentuated, lift with both, lower with one

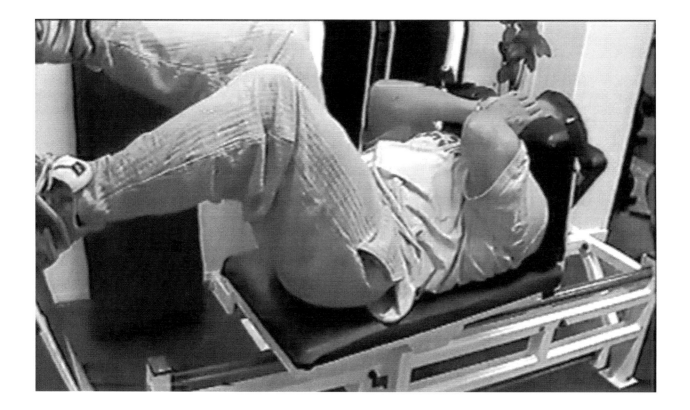

This log diary is perhaps the most boring here, but what it does show is a steady training weight progression, from starting squats to the last entries there is a huge difference – over the weeks here and over 40kg added to it. Also all other exercises had a similar corresponding improvement. The intensity was high – I pushed so hard and boy did I grow eventually I ate over 5000 calories a day and topped out at 12 stone 7lb or so, 174 – 175lb.

Also note the foods are varied and nothing fancy at all, just lots of it – more carbs than anything else.

Study these pages if you want to undergo this HIT program. Study and adapt to yourself, train hard get stronger and eat a calorie surplus to gain, it's simple. Not easy but simple, the hard part is the training as it should be – go for it.

Summer 2007

Pro Am Training – British Guest Pose – Worlds

What a year this was – I had really started to come in to my own by now, takes me a long time to get good at something, but I never give up. I will have been 43 or so here.

I start the entries for you guys 6 weeks out from the Pro Am – this week we were away at Centre Parcs and I had trained with just a couple of dumbbells and bands I took with me. This year through the off season and into the prep I followed a very heavy basic AST type program.

I was sponsored by AST – the American company that also sponsored one of the top naturals of the world, Skip Lacour. I was and still am very inspired by Skip and looked to his type of programs for inspiration. It was not dissimilar to what I am doing now, six to nine sets major body parts, three to six smaller ones.

As the weeks progressed I got tighter and tighter – I reduced the volume bit by bit till I was doing a split HIT type program, this worked fantastic in the last few weeks of the show prep – by the time I reached the Worlds I was in at that point the best shape of my life.

Reducing the volume and increasing the intensity added fullness and even more condition.

This year went Pro Am win, Guest Spot at the British for the ANB, very few have done so, and was over the moon to be asked.

Then I went on to the Worlds and won that also.

The next time I was on stage was 2009 – that story follows, with lots of notes.

Monday 20 August 2007

Away in Centre Parcs. Look better than I ever have done in my life. Tight in my back, chest, triceps, bloody everywhere Louise said she has never seen my delts or back like it is now.

Ace.

Tuesday 21 August 2007

Walking loads

Wednesday 22 August 2007

Stick with these carbs in diet for a few weeks to get sharper, want to be my best ever condition.

Need more off my lower back so need to come down more don't care what I weigh as long as I am shredded.

Practiced posing, 6 weeks to go.

Thursday 23 August 2007

Chins in morning, afternoon back and biceps, abs

Friday 24 August 2007

Back home – 148 look very good will be better

Saturday 25 August 2007

No entry

Sunday 26 August 2007

Diet change more fats, Skip Lacour. Vision this year need to be best ever. Best ever.

Monday 26 August 2007

No entry

Tuesday 28 August 2007

Tuesday 28 August 2007
Floor press 37.5kg, 10, 6
Incline flyes 27.5, bench press 20kg plus 15kg, 5, 5
Rack press 30kg, dips 25kg, 10, 6
Band press, 15, 15
Lat raise 30kg, 12, 10
Rack press 17.5, dumbbell press 6, 4, 30kg 2 sets each
Bent over lat raise 32.5, 30kg 12, 12
Close press 27.5, extensions 15kg, 12, 8
Pulldowns and band, pushdowns 80kg, 10, 10 - band

Wednesday 29 August 2007

This diet change has worked awesome, look very very sharp. Busy day had two bars extra.

Thursday 30 August 2007

Pre workout drink coffee post workout 3 hours. *Note – 3 hour post workout was one post workout drank right after workout then I did two more, 1 hour apart then a meal at 3 hour mark.

Chins 20kg + 5kg, 5, 6, 2 plates + 5kg, 6, 5

Bent over rows 3 plates 8, 8

Power shrugs 2 plates + 7.5kg 10, 10

Band rows 15, 15 *Note – I was using TNT bands almost every workout – still use them a lot today.

Curls thick bar 7.5kg + 1 1/4 , 10, 8

Seated 22, 10, 7

Band 8, 6

Abs

*Note – I always work out weights by what is on each side of the bar – not total kg or pounds

Friday 31 August 2007

Looking very very sharp, best ever

Saturday 1 September 2007

Leg extensions 190, 15, 15

Leg curls seated, 15, 15

Squat 3 plates + 7.5kg 15, 11

Leg curls 9 plates, 15, 12

Band squats 20, 20

Stiff leg 85kg, 20, 20

Power lunge 20, 20

Toe press 190kg (knock hell out of them)

Band calf raise to fail

Abs

Sunday 2 September 2007

No entry

Monday 3 September 2007

No entry

Tuesday 4 September 2007

Floor press 37.5kg 12, 9 – Dumbbell Chest Press on floor

Incline flyes 27.5, 10

Rack press 30kg, 10, 7 – Bench Press in rack off pins

Band press 15, 15

Lat raise 30kg, 12, 12

Rack press 17.5, 12, 10 – Shoulder Press in rack off pins

Bent over lat raise 32.5, 12, 16

Close press 27.5, extensions 15kg, 12, 10

Band pushdowns to fail

Wednesday 5 September 2007

Super busy day, had no veg with Nytro extra at night

Thursday 6 September 2007

Chins 2 plates + 5kg, 7, 6

Bent over rows 3 plates, 10 , 8

Power shrugs, 2 plates + 10kg, 17

Band rows, 15, 15

Curls thick 10kg, 8, 7

Seated 22.5kg, 10, 10

Band curl, 12, 10

Abs

Awesome workout look very very sharp, better than I have ever been in my life. I want to win this last show of my career bad. Want to win.

Friday 7 September 2007

Note - I was very strong at this point in my life and lean as well. Back especially. 3 plate bent over rows and 2 plates added around my waist on chins.

Legs in afternoon

Leg extension 195, 15, 15, with leg curls seated 105, 15, 12

Squats rack 10 holes 3 plates + 10kg, 12, 10

Leg curls 9 plates, 12, 11 with front hacks 25 a side 20, 15

Stiff leg 85kg, 20, 15 with power lunge – high, 15, 15 *Jumping scissor lunge

Toe press

Saturday 8 September 2007

Great day Sam 2nd

Sunday 9 September 2007

Ace day again did loads with kids and business plans

Monday 10 September 2007

Put banana in and 50g of spud back at lunch all other same

Look loads better today very sharp very full

Tuesday 11 September 2007

Floor press 40kg, 8, 6

Incline rack 30kg + 1 1/4 , bench press 20kg + 15kg, 8, 5

Incline flyes 30kg, 8, 6

Bands press 15, 15

*Lat raise 32.5kg, 8, 6

Rack press 20kg, free 8, 6

Bent over lat raise 35kg, 8, 8

Extensions 16.5kg, 10, 9

Band pushdowns and dips 15, 10

Rack in use today

*Note – I had spent almost a year building up the lat raise to over 30kg dumbbells – it worked wonders. Giving me much more delt thickness.

Wednesday 12 September 2007

1	Oats 2oz	180		45
	Whey	104	24	
	Banana	100		20
2	½ Nytro	120	20	15
	Whey	104	20	
	Veg	50		10
	Oil	110		
3	Chicken	230	36	
	Spud	228		51
	Veg	50		10
	Oil	110		
4	½ Nytro	120	20	
	Whey	104	20	
	Veg	50		10
	Oil	110		
5	Chicken	230	36	
	Veg	50		10
	Oil	110		
6	½ Nytro	120	20	15
	Whey	104	20	
		2384	216	186

Lowered carbs slightly again ½ meal replacement and added whey – this gave same meal size, half the carbs. This was my baseline plan as of this time.

Thursday 13 September 2007

Chins 2 plates + 5kg, 7, 6

Bent rows 3 plates + 2 1/2 , 8, 6

Power shrug 2 plates + 2 1/2 , 10, 10

Band rows 15, 15

Curls thick 10kg, 10, 6

Seated 25kg, 8, 7

Band curls

Abs (side bends) and hanging leg raise plus twists

Friday 14 September 2007

No entry

Saturday 15 September 2007

Legs

Leg extensions 205, 15, 15 with leg curls 110, 12, 18

Squat 3 plates + 12 ½ 12, 8

Leg curls 10 plates, 12, 10, with front hacks 30kg, 15, 15

Stiff legs 50kg dumbbells with walking lunges

Toe press

Sunday 16 September 2007

Felt drained today very very tired, that workout yesterday
Made some carrot cake and muffins for kids and Lou
Look shredded

Monday 17 September 2007

Fair busy day felt tired still but came round later on

Tuesday 18 September 2007

Floor press, 40kg 10, 7
Bench 20kg plus 15kg 7, 5
Incline flyes 9, 7
Band press 15, 15
Lat raise 32.5, 8, 8, drop 15kg x 10
Front press 20kg press dumbbell and twist 25kg 5, 7
Bent over lat raise 35kg 15kg, 12, 12
Extensions 16 ¼ 10, 9
Pushdowns

Wednesday 19 September 2007

Busy busy day
No pose today save energy for workout

Thursday 20 September 2007

Feel ace look good, very happy
Chins 2 plates + 5kg 8, 5
Bent row 3 plates + 2 ½ 8, 7
Power shrugs 2 plates + 15kg x 10
Band rows 20, 25
Curls 10 thick bar EZ bar instead 17.5kg 12, 12
Seated 25kg, 9, 8
Band
Abs

Friday 21 September 2007

No entry

Heavy Incline Curls – photo training partner Paul Twig

Andy Barber in the background checking his journal

Saturday 22 September 2007

Legs

Leg extensions 100kg x 15, holding for 5 seconds at top

2 sets 15, 12

Squats rack off pins 3 plates x 10 reps tense at top for 5 secs 2 x 10 no belt

Tensing like hell

Front kicks cable 2 plates 2 x 15

Stretching and tensing

Leg curls 6 plates, 2 x 15

Rear kicks 2 plates, 2 x 12

Tense and squeeze

Sunday 23 September 2007

No entry

Monday 24 September 2007

Less than 2 weeks now, foods and sups

1. Oats 2oz, 1 banana and 1 scoop whey

2. ½ Nytro 1 scoop whey salad and oil

3. 250g spud, turkey 200g, 400 cals – 52g pro, salad, oil, 2 spoon 100 cals

4. ½ Nytro 1 scoop whey salad and oil

6. ½ Nytro 1 scoop whey

Training days keep same format

Replaced chicken for turkey its more cals but lower in fats and sodium

Changed veg for a salad

Approx cals 2268

Tuesday 25 September 2007

Floor press 40kg 10, 7

Bench press 20kg + 15kg 6, 5

Incline flyes 30kg, 8

Cross overs, 15, 15, 4 plates

Lat raise 32.5, drop 15kg 8, 8

Dumbbell press 25kg, 10, 8

Bent over lat raise 15kg, 15, 15

Extensions 17.5, 8, 6

Pushdowns – 60kg, 10, 10

Abs

Wednesday 26 September 2007

Legs

Squats 3 plates deep, 2 x 10

1 leg, leg press 4 plates, 3 x 20

1 leg, leg extension 55kg, 2 x 15

Leg curls 6 plates, 15, 12, 12 with ball rear squeeze on swiss ball 20, 20, 20

Toe press 5 x 20 6 plates

Thursday 27 September 2007

Chins 2 plates + 5kg, 10, 7
Bent over rows 3 plates + 7.5kg, 10, 8
Power shrugs 2 plates + 15kg, 10, 10
Band rows 15, 15, standing
Curls thick 10kg, 10, 6
Seated 25kg, 10
Band
Abs
Felt absolutely wasted today so tired
But on the good side look absolutely shredded, Mick Philips came to see me, foods are bang on

Friday 28 September 2007

Foods the same

Saturday 29 September 2007

Here's my plan
1. Oats – normal
2. Meal replacement ½ whey and oil
3 Turkey, spud and normal veg and oil
4. Turkey and salad and oil
5. Meal replacement ½ whey and oil
Wine
*Note – meal replacement was AST Nytro Pro 40 and whey was VyoPro also by AST

Sunday 30 September 2007

1. Oats normal
2. ½ meal and whey and oil
3. Whey pro x 2 oil and a spud
4. ½ meal and whey and oil
5. ½ meal and why and oil
6. ½ meal and whey and oil
Check list
All together and meals whey and meal replacements 7.
I was away at shows and this was the plan away from home, I had a lot of clients that competed.
1. Bring 2 wheys for lunch
2. Turkey meals one with spud at bed one without
1. Oat meal to take
2. Pack of meal replacement just in case

Monday 1 October 2007

The plan with foods work was awesome look freaky
Had an hour 20 mins of sleep went to work

Tuesday 2 October 2007

Floor press 40kg 10, 7
Bench press 20kg + 15kg 5, 5
Flyes 30kg, 8, 7
Lat raise drop sets 22.5kg, 10, 15kg 10, 10
Dumbbell press 25kg
Bent over head on bench lat raise 27.5kg, 10, 10
Extensions 17.5kg, 8, 8
Pushdowns
Abs
Foods good

Wednesday 3 October 2007

Chins 2 sets
Dumbbell row 2 sets
Shrugs 2 sets
Low rows 2 sets
Curls bar 2 sets
Seated curls 2 sets
Side bends leg raise
Busy day today
Train back light ish with plenty of squeeze
Got a sunbed as well
use this day as a workout day – food wise
3 litres water
Foods
1. Whey and HSC
2. Whey and HSC rice cakes
3. Whey and HSC rice cakes
4. Oats and Nytro
5. Turkey spud and veg, oil
6. ½ Nytro and whey
7. Turkey and veg, oil

Thursday 4 October 2007

Plan
1. Oats 2oz, banana and whey
2. ½ Nytro 1 whey, 2 spoon oil, veg and ½ baked spud
3. Turkey 200g, veg, 2 spoon oil, ½ baked spud
4. ½ Nytro and whey, ½ baked spud, veg, 2 spoons oil
5. Turkey 200g, veg, 2 spoon oil, ½ baked spud
6. ½ Nytro 1 whey
2 ½ spuds total
2 litres water

Friday 5 October 2007

Look awesome – shredded and rested, keep cool and win - win

1. Oats 2oz, banana and whey
2. ½ Nytro 1 whey, 2 spoon oil
3. Turkey 200g, veg, 2 spoon oil, 250g baked spud
4. ½ Nytro and whey, 2 spoons oil
5. Turkey 200g, veg, 2 spoon oil, 200g baked spud
6. ½ Nytro 1 whey

Wine

2 spuds total

2 litres water and a little less

1 ½ litre and a green tea

Saturday 6 October 2007

Plan

1. 3oz oats and banana and whey

*2. ½ Nytro 1 whey, 2 spoon oil, 2 rice cakes

Every 3 hours

Chocolate and wine back stage, had an egg sarnie and chocolate on way home water as needed it

Cornflakes at night ha-ha – I won.

*I did this up to 1 hour before stage and had dark chocolate and wine. It worked a treat – the rice cakes were snack-a-jacks, caramel ones.

Sunday 7 October 2007

Off day eat what I want today

Monday 8 October 2007

Here we go okay

Plan

1. 3oz oats instead of 2, banana and whey
2. Pud mix and veg and oil
3. Turkey or chicken spud 250g, veg and oil
4. Turkey veg and oil
5. Pud mix and oil

*Note – pud mix is the Nytro and whey mix I was doing

Training days keep the same

Tuesday 9 October 2007

Workout 1

Leg extension 2 sets

squat 2 sets

Leg press 1 leg 2 sets

Leg curls 2 sets

Front kicks 2 sets

Workout 2

Chest

Bench press 20kg + 15kg 2 x 6

Incline dumbbell 32.5kg 2 x 10

Dips 30kg 2 x 10

Shoulder press 20kg 2 x 10

Lat raise drop sets 2 sets

Rear machine 2 sets

Extensions 2 sets

Pushdowns 2 sets

Abs

Wednesday 10 October 2007

Mega busy day

Work it hard

Be professional

Thursday 11 October 2007

Chins 30kg 2 x 10

T Bar 3 plates 10 , 10

Deadlifts 3 plates, 8

Shrugs 32kg 2 x 15

Rows cable 70kg 2 x 15

Rows cable 130kg 1 x 12

Curls 10kg thick bar 2 x 12

Seated alternate 22kg, 7, 7 each

Band curls 2 x 10

Abs

Friday 12 October 2007

No entry

Saturday 13 October 2007

Legs

8 holes – rack squats 3 plates, 6, 6

Front hacks 30kg a side, 20, 20

1 leg, leg press 4 plates total 2 x 20

Leg curls 6 ½ plates 15, 12

Toe press 250kg drop 160kg – 100kg, 2 drop sets 15, 12 reps

Hard workout (not a killer) but hard on my own 14:50 – 15:25

Look mega tight veins in every inch of my body just freaky now

Sunday 14 October 2007

Okay this week

2oz oats

200g spud

Till Thursday

200g turkey a meal

Keep oil same

Just veg lunch and night

Monday 15 October 2007

Went to work at 04:00 wrote HIT article and spoke on email too Bill Piche Cyberpump

Very busy day and productive

Also my photo and log was on DrDarden.com the HIT site

Ace day

Tuesday 16 October 2007

Again 03:30 up coffee and meal, both the gym

Chest and back

- Bench press 2 sets 10, 8
- Incline flyes 2 sets 22.5kg, 12, 10
- Dips 2 sets no weight

- Deadlifts 3 plates, 8, 8
- Chins 12, 8
- Dumbbell rows

Shrugs

Abs

Wednesday 17 October 2007

04:30

Delts and arms fail

Lat raise 15kg, press machine 130kg fail, rear machine fail, lat raise again fail

Curls 10kg fail, chins underhand fail, curls seated fail

Extensions 10kg fail, pushdowns 65kg to fail, dips to fail

Foods same on workout days

Decided to do Worlds after I spoke to Louise

Thursday 18 October 2007

Same as last Thursday before show

½ spud extra each meal

Look just out of this world for me, striations through out every part of me

Triceps and back and arse just shredded

Friday 19 October 2007

Same plan

Saturday 20 October 2007

Guest posed and British

Same plan foods all same, 2 hours chocolate and wine

Didn't cheat too much on the night had fruit cake and few biscuits and sweets

Sunday 21 October 2007

Cheat breakfast eggs and toast, cereal

Monday 22 October 2007

Back to diet, keep same

3oz oats, 250g spud this week

Same workout days

Drop few carbs again next week, follow plan

Tuesday 23 October 2007

Leg extension 145 x 12, 2 forced

Squat 3 plates deep and slow x 10

Hacks 3 plates deep and slow x 12

Leg curls 8 plates 10 + 2

Single leg curl 40kg, 2 x 10

Toe press 205kg 2 x 10

Curls 10kg thick x 11

Pushdown 12kg x 8

Extensions 12.5kg x 14

Pushdowns 65kg x 10

Abs

Awesome workout

Wednesday 24 October 2007

No entry

Thursday 25 October 2007

Bench press 20kg + 10kg + 1 1/4 , 10 + 2

Incline flyes 25kg x 12

Dips 20kg x 10

Band 12

Chins 25kg 8 + 2F, drop 5

Bent over rows 2 plates + 10kg, 10

Deadlifts 3 plates + 5kg, 9

Lat raise 20kg x 12, 15kg x 6

Press rack, 20kg thick 12 + 2

Bent over lat 20kg x 14

Upright row 30kg x 14

Abs

Moved up to 3 litre water looked a little flat but very sharp but when tensed felt dead in muscles

There wasn't that boom so water up to 3

Friday 26 October 2007

No entry

Saturday 27 October 2007

Extra traps and abs, and calves in morning

Sunday 28 October 2007

Reduce

200g spud, 2 oz oats, 1 spoon oil, each meal

Till Thursday, ad spuds up again oil and oats

Monday 29 October 2007

Foods ace as always

Tuesday 30 October 2007

Workout - filmed DVD

Part One

Looking very good better than both shows today, very very sharp look full chest is best ever. Routine is good, high intensity

Wednesday 31 October 2007

No entry

Thursday 1 November 2007

No entry

Friday 2 November 2007

Away in Madrid

Took loads and I mean loads of Vyo pro bars with me as getting food was hard

I still kept to my diet as listed weeks ago

Pud mix was Vyo Pro and a Nytro pro 40 ½ and half mix

This I ate almost exclusively while away along with bars

These were AST products very good stuff

This dried me out and kept me very full. After the show, loads of people wanted to know about AST products before a show

Saturday 3 November

Worlds – I won, John third

Spring 2009

Probably the best I have ever looked – and I did this for a Guest Pose at the Yorkshire Championships, an absolute honour to be asked and it was just an awesome day.

Lots of learning curves this year that I still implement to this day, just let me back up a bit.

In 2008, I flew to LA to spend a week with one of the best bodybuilders on the planet, Robby Robinson.

Time With The Master Robby Robinson

Day 1- Sun 21st Sept 2008

I got up at my normal time of 04:00, had a bath and a shave and got dressed, all the while trying not to disturb the family. Stood in the kitchen eating an oatcake and drinking a strong black coffee, my mind settled on the sort of mixed feelings I was having. Yes, I was excited for my trip and I anticipated all I would absorb and be able to use in the future, but I also felt sad that my family was not going with me.

What with the kids in school and Louise not being able to have time off work I would be travelling alone. Chris, my old buddy came round for me, to take me to Manchester Airport. After leaving the family a note, I popped my bags in the boot and I was on my way, the start of a long journey.

Everything went smoothly, the airport check ins and other what not's all went fine and I was soon on a Virgin Atlantic flight bound for LAX Airport- with 11 hours of flying ahead, I am glad that they let me on the plane with my trusty oatcakes. I used the time to read (as always) and to write some business goals and a new business structure. I have a ton of ideas and goals and they all need a structure, otherwise they get lost between the ears and never see the light of day, so I sat and dissected each and every one. Yes, I will improve my business further with this trip, but I will also get time to look after me.

Believe it or not, being the top trainer that I am, I am very busy. This leaves little time for 'me'. I try to give to family and clients and this makes for really unsociable hours of working out. It's work at 4:50am, train at 5:30am, work by 6:15am. I can only do my own training 3 days a week tops; as with all the hours and how active I am there would be no recovery time. So this week will be a chance to train when I want, eat good food and not rush around. To relax after a workout for a little while- never happens- so it will be a nice change- watch me be bored, ha-ha.

The Meeting with Robby

When the plane landed, feelings of apprehension built up in me, knowing I was going to meet with someone very famous in our world. After a lengthy, drawn out customs procedure I claimed my bags and moved outside into the street level of LAX Airport.

Soon after a black Ford jeep pulls up and out steps Robby and his partner Arden. Robby just grabs my hand and gives me a hug, and then so does Arden, who is tall and elegant with long blonde hair. Robby-who is dressed in a black long sleeved t-shirt and trousers – looks muscular, sleek and athletic. The way he moves defies his age.

One of the first things I noticed about Robby is his impeccable manners- as he even walks round to open the car door for Arden. Where has that gone? (Louise and I were only talking about that the other day- another article perhaps.) After a chat about the flight and what not, Robby says, "Let's get you something to eat."

In a shot we are at The Firehouse, a very famous restaurant that caters for bodybuilders, and it is walking distance from the famous Gold's Gym. I sat there tucking into my buffalo pate and rice and veg. Chatting along with this lovely couple, with the sun blazing outside just blew my mind. One minute it seemed I was in bed at home and the next I'm here. Very surreal.

The Master And Pupil

Later Robby and Arden dropped me off at the Foghorn Harbor Inn. A beautiful little hotel-that overlooks the marina and has a beach right on its doorstep. Just beautiful, I checked in and made my way to my room. After unpacking I decided to go for a walk. Just heading out of the door Robby calls on the phone to ask if everything is ok and if I am settled. I thank him and he says, "I will pick you up in the morning for a workout."

Oh yeah, I thought, I'm going to train with the man!!!

I spent a good two hours walking and getting my bearings. I have been here twice before and can vaguely remember how to get about. Being a coffee lover, I searched out the nearest Starbucks. I found one not far from the beachfront and went in to get my fix and was amazed to find you can get a shot of protein in it. I didn't, but I got a coffee to take out and walked around with it to look all American like

My Room Was Right On The Front x

Day 2 – Workout 1

Very little sleep as always, I spent the night looking at the clock and was excited at the prospect of the day ahead. After a breakfast of oats, honey and protein powder I headed onto the beach with my bag of books and writing pad. As I write and look out at the view, a young lad behind me in the parking area conducts a boot camp style workout.

What a life, eh?

After writing and planning- time, income and the sale of the new DVD- I took a walk around the marina. As I headed around the Marina I came across Marina Fitness Gym- with a fitness café below it. This once again was overlooking the marina. I looked at my watch –time was going real slow—time for something to eat though, so headed in the cafe

I ordered oats and egg whites-the menu on the wall called it- Lou's Special- like my little man I thought. As I sat overlooking the Marina eating this, I thought about how health orientated is this. Anybody who cares about the way they look and if their life is built around 'the iron'. – "You Must Come Here."

It's Disneyland for the bodybuilder and fitness enthusiast.

Around lunchtime Robby and Arden picked me up and we headed to Marina Fitness- right above where I had a meal earlier. First we sat outside for 5-10 minutes, where upon Arden filmed Robby and myself talking about training, nutrition and supplements. This ended up being quite extensive and deep. We then headed into the gym for a Shoulders and Arms workout.

This was to be a Giant Set type workout, thereby going from one exercise to another. I have always prided myself on being able to put myself in a position of muscle stimulation, but Robby took me to another level. The setting up of my body prior to movement was a big factor and staying there through the entire set, is what killed you.

Here is what we did, the entire session lasted around 45 minutes:

Standing Front Press for delts, Seated Lat Raise, Bent Over Lat Raise, Close Grip Press, Curls, Overhead Cable Pushouts, Cable Curls. We then started the whole process again with a little more weight; the aim was 12 reps on the first round, 8-10 on the second, then 6 on the third. I could not believe how much I could feel the muscle with the prompting from Robby on form.

The entire workout was filmed as were the others and some of it will be on Robby's site, then for sale soon after. The filming is something I will have to do with my clients in the future as you can only absorb so much at once and the luxury of having a DVD to watch time and time again will allow you to soak up as much as possible. Knowledge is power and you can never learn enough or know it all- never stop learning.

After the workout, we had a post workout drink of juice, glutamine and flax oil and then headed off for some much needed food. Robby and Arden took me to the farmers market. This I was blown away by- rows upon rows of organic natural foods. One part of the store had a point in which you picked some meat and it was cooked for you while you waited- I picked buffalo pate again, Robby a beef skewer and Arden a chicken skewer. We then purchased rice and veg from other departments and sat down to eat it.

Like I said it is a bodybuilders' Disneyland.

Later Robby and Arden dropped me back at the hotel and I had time to reflect. It was just an awesome day- learnt a lot- trained hard and enjoyed every minute.

I cannot wait till tomorrow's Chest and Back workout.

Day 3 – Workout 2

I awake with a start on the day. Right away I took my morning supplements that Robby had structured out for me for the days ahead, I washed these down with cold, clean water. After morning rituals I headed out for breakfast at the Marina Fitness café. I had the usual- oats, egg whites and blueberries with a black coffee and more supplements.

I will write more about supplements at another time when I know more about their role in how Robby has structured them. After that awesome breakfast I was ready for anything. I was scheduled to meet Robby and Arden at 9am for Chest and Back work after which they planned to take me to the Santa Monica Stairs, all 198 of them going all the way up and of course down. With the time I had between breakfast and the workout I headed to the beach to do a little more writing.

The Workout

We hooked up outside the gym and once again did a little filming before heading inside for the workout. Chest and Back was the order of the day. Here is what we did:

To start with we did an exercise that Robby has done for years for opening out the lats, hard to explain, but it is a little like a vacuum pose. I found this exercise a lot harder on the muscles than it looked. But thought it would be fantastic for those clients that struggle with a lat spread and the front relaxed pose, as it really helped you open up. After a little band work for posture.

We then move to Low Pulley Rows using a handle that Robby explained was used by all the greats in the sport – Arnold, Edd Corney, Zane, the original Gold's gang- and it was made by Joe Gold himself. It made the Low Rows even more special, I tell you, knowing the history behind the bar. We did these much different to what I had done in the past and I felt them really deep in the whole of my lat. We did one set of 12-15 reps. Again guys all this will be available on the DVD.

We then moved to Dead lifts in the rack. Again style was the main focus and correct body mechanics at all times, we did a set each of ten reps. Chest was up next- Robby expressed that he was a great fan of Vince Gironda and had always wanted to train with him but never got the chance. Robby also said he has used some of Vince's techniques for many years.

Hence we moved on to a Flat Bench Neck Press-like a bench press but the bar travels more towards the upper peck neck area. This will place the stress a little more on the upper pec area. We did a set each with a weight that allowed 12 reps.

Next up we did a Dumbbell Flat Bench Press for 12 reps, very strict movement with a hard contraction and a deep stretch. Over the years I have read in articles 'squeeze the contraction, feel the movement, concentrate'– and I have done that, but not on this level. I had been well and truly schooled.

We then headed back through the gym to the Low Pulley Row, with the priceless handle in tow. In fact it went everywhere with us, it was like another training partner. We add weight and Robby again went through a picture perfect set and then made sure I got a perfect set also by constantly- encouraging and correcting- "Come on Ian, I'm going to get my reps, make me work now, come on"- in that deep unmistakable voice. I got 10 reps here.

Then it was back to Dead Lifts, with again a little more on the bar. We followed this up with Neck Press again, a little more weight, a little more feel and even better reps- 10 reps each. Dumbbell Press next –yes you are getting the sequence, 10 reps again.

After this we did two sets of Pullover and Press- 85lbs for Set One and 75lbs for Set Two with an even deeper stretch. This was a great movement that I felt in the lats and chest. This was the hardest movement for me, as Robby demanded a deep; deep stretch hence the lighter weight on the second set. We finished up the workout with a set of Chins.

All the time that I had spent with Robby and Arden I had never seen any of Robby's physique, he constantly wore a Built T shirt, sometimes two- and a vest. With a little prompting from Arden and myself he took his tops off in the studio room. As you can see from the shots, he looks fantastic- this is Robby's everyday look, a physique that is built with good clean foods and clean living and training. Drugs in the sport were responsible for a very small part of his bodybuilding efforts, he built his size the natural way and that's why today at 62, yes he is 62 in these photos, he looks like he does.

After a post workout drink in the Jeep, we headed for the Santa Monica steps. These famous steps were situated in the Santa Monica Valley. I was surprised to see a horde of people on them- some even held light dumbbells and pumped away with their arms as they went up and down them. We parked at the top and headed all the way down the 198 steps, and then we began the climb.

They were very steep and it really got stuck into the hips, glutes and calves. Robby and myself did a round then Arden, then it was Robby and I again followed by Arden. This was followed by an ice-cold regulator drink with added Glutamine by Robby and Arden. Everything was taken care of. This was something they did to a fault- they looked after me like you wouldn't believe. They were very thoughtful and caring- the passion for this- just jumps out at you.

Drinking the ice cold post workout drink and looking out over the valley, was just heaven and it was a beautiful day. After that fantastic workout and stair climb it was time for another meal. Robby and Arden knew of just the spot. They took me to a beautiful little restaurant that is frequented by Hollywood stars and sports celebs whereupon we ordered and tucked into a 'Trainer's Special' as the menu said- egg whites, rice, fruit and whole-wheat pancakes.

In between eating, we filmed a little more and covered subjects like- business- and how I train the BodyIndesign girls, also how incredibly strong they are. Robby also talked about competing and how people should not do long duration CV- this I smiled at, as I have been banging on about not doing CV for a long time now.

After this delicious meal we headed to their home, as Arden has some things there for me. My eyes lit up upon seeing a draft copy (that nobody else has yet seen outside of the family) of Robby's biography book The Black Prince. This I was very humbled by. I was also given a watermelon and some low salt, low yeast bread bought from the farmer's market that they visit regularly.

They then dropped me off back at my hotel. After a shower I headed out to my favorite spot for writing. Sat in the sun, I reflected on the day as I wrote the piece you have just read. I watched the sun go down on an awesome day and was excited at what was in-store tomorrow.

Day 4 – off day from training

After breakfast, a little walk and phoning home Robby and Arden picked me up. They took me to an organic market in Santa Monica where they buy their food supplies. This was paradise again for me- row after row of fresh from the farm foods as Robby put it.

Robby went off shopping and Arden and I went off in another direction. This gave me the chance to have a nice chat with her about how much I think Robby is grounded with her. Behind every great man there is a great woman and she is no exception. You can see the love and respect these two people have for each other. He is constantly the gentleman with her. So you guys out there tell your girl that you love em and appreciate all that they do for you. You never realise what you have- till it's gone.

After the market Robby and Arden took me to a store where Robby buys the herbs that he uses in this master plan. He picked them out for me and Arden and I weighed them. Herbs, Robby explains, are something that have been used for many hundreds of years and are something he has always used himself.

We bagged up about seven and he said he would take them home and ground them up for me then drop them off later and show me how to structure their use. I was looking forward to this because in only 3 days I could see a difference in my physique. Some of this is due to rest, as I don't normally stop, but most definitely some of this is also due to the advanced balance of supplements and training, with good food also of course.

I came out here in good shape, I never lose my abs, but I lacked a little muscle fullness and was not as vascular as normal. But now I looked full and hard. My skin also looked better from the use of oils Robby had given me to try out. This is something I had been concerned about as I am now 42 and my skin is not as tight as it was when I was younger.

Robby gave me the oils he uses. Yes, he is black- and genetically he would not age as much as a white guy – having said that he is 62 and looks under 40. There is only so much that is genetic. I thought it was just genetic but having spoken at length about this I found that- no-he works at it- he looks after himself. He uses oils for his face when shaving and oils his body many times a day; also the right supplements are used for anti-ageing.

Sure enough later, around noon, Robby came by with the packs of herbs and told me the best times to use them for the best effects. He also said he had a surprise for me and had ordered a cab to take us there. We headed to downtown LA to Wiltshire BLVD for a Pilates session. Robby had booked me in with a young lady he uses often for body alignment, Miki Muller. For the next 45 minutes Miki put me through a series of movements to work deep into the core of my body and lengthen my spine. All the while Robby laughed at me-"Work that man, make him have it Miki." She had me in positions I didn't know I could do and I like to think I fared well. The positions plus the breathing exercises made me feel relaxed and deep down worked all at the same time. She was very good and very professional and knew the body inside out- Robby told me later that she is the best there is and anybody who is anybody goes to her; she's the best in the USA.

Visit with Dean

Now here was a whole new world of experience for me. Dean was featured in Robby's Built DVD and everything that was done here today was filmed for the Master Plan DVD featuring all that Robby, Arden and I did over this week. I say that because the session I had here was so advanced that I would have to write a book, to even touch on the work here. So I will cover in brief and you can see the footage yourself.

Dean is what you call a body mechanics master; his knowledge is off the charts. Basically he worked on the fascia tissue of the body and released it, so perfect body mechanics could be used and therefore allowing more efficient movement, range of motion and even distribution of load. Robby was first on the table and I watched as he got extreme ranges of motion from him all the while explaining what he was doing and why. Dean is a huge guy and Robby was putty in his hands.

After Robby it was my turn, I was filled with a bit of apprehension. Dean stood and looked at me- I wondered what he was looking at and looked behind me. This got a laugh from everyone. Basically he was checking me out, lining me up in his mind. When I stood I had one hip further forward than the other. Heavy dead lifts had twisted me so my right side was forward and up from the hip region. When I laid on the table, I was worked and manipulated from many angles that you just have to see to believe the range of motion that he got in my shoulders- it freaked me out. A fantastic experience worth the DVD price alone as you will learn so much about the human body and it's workings.

Later on that day I decided I would have a walk to The Firehouse for a meal. The mechanics work made me feel so good, my body was like a fine tuned machine and as fluid as water itself. I could not believe how good I felt, walking along the beachfront. This is just an awesome vacation and learning experience all in one.

Before heading in for a meal I called into Gold's. I as having a look around the shop there for some trackies and heard a voice "Hey are you Ian Duckett?" Yes it's true, I kid you not. All the bloody way out here and I bump into two great English lads who's names escape me (so guys I know you read my blogs so please email me so I can keep in contact).

We had a chat and they said they had seen me win the Pro Am last year and we took photos- this I was so humbled by as there we are with the world's best bodybuilders around us and they want to talk to me and take photos. Thank you guys, you made my day even more special. Later when I sat in the Firehouse I wished I had asked them to join me. Hope you enjoyed your stay guys and your trip to the Olympia.

Day 5 –Legs

I always think that the mark of a bodybuilder is how he can train his legs. You have to have a certain kind of mental strength to develop good legs. In my time I have done my fair share of hard legwork and I looked forward to what Robby had in store for me. Meeting Robby and Arden at the gym- Arden wanted to run through some back stretches for me after my work with Dean yesterday. Just prior to that, we had another interview outside covering the last four days work.

As we started the workout with some ab work, Robby showed me a great exercise I had never done before or even seen. It was very effective and I could feel it in the whole length of my abs. After 4 sets of this they were toasted and we moved on to.

Legs

We started out with Leg Extensions and combined these with Leg Curls. Robby was- as always- a stickler for style. He also explained his visualisation techniques. Reps were performed in a machine like style, picture perfect. We did one set each of 15 reps and moved to Leg Press with 4 plates a side for 15 reps each. Robby had me perform these nice and deep, slow and controlled with constant tension. We then went back to Leg Extensions and Leg Curls with a little more weight and around 12 reps each. Back to the Leg Press with 6 plates a side for 12 reps and then added another 2 plates taking it up to 8 plates a side for 10 reps. These were very tough to do right and a lot more painful.

It was then back to the extensions and Leg Curls, these were the hardest sets with a hard contraction at the completion of each rep. Robby made sure I got the reps and in picture perfect style, as always. It's amazing how hard you will work, when one of the world's best bodybuilders and legends is encouraging you to do one more rep.

Calves were next up with 4 sets of Seated Calf Raises with the magic Robby difference. He demanded a deep, deep stretch and a high, high contraction squeezing like mad. It had been a few years since I had used a Seated Calf Machine and it bit really deep. I knew I would be in pain in the morning.

I really enjoyed this workout and I had absorbed once again, a world of information and felt it also. After such work Robby said we needed to eat, so off we went to The Firehouse for some Buffalo, rice and veg. Hard work and good food, a large part of Robby's master plan.

Day 5

We planned to do interviews today for the DVD so after a visit to another fresh market whereupon Robby and Arden introduced me to Wheatgrass. This they have once a week- shot like- like in an alcoholic shot- but this being way better for you. The green liquid looked like swamp water and I didn't relish the taste of it, or much- like the look of it. Robby had two and Arden one- so I was in a corner- yep down it went- actually it was ok and tasted like sugar snap peas. Apparently very good as an antioxidant and has many other properties.

We headed down to the beach near my hotel for an interview, regarding all we had done over the past few days. I must say we covered tons here. Robby talked about the old days, his training now and then, his philosophies, his goals and also mine. We had a real good chat and a laugh. Robby was in great form and he always, always impresses me.

After saying goodbye for that day, I set off into Santa Monica via the bus system that was an adventure in itself. I wanted to do a little shopping before heading home in a couple of days. I had some money of Heather's burning a hole in my pocket and I wanted some new clothes for myself. I was the typical guy, in one shop I bought it all and was out and done. Bing- bang- bosh- I don't mess about with shopping.

When I got back to my room I headed out for some food at the Marina Café just down from my hotel. Yep it's work is this; hope you feel sorry for me. I ordered egg whites, avocado and veg in a whole meal wrap- it was awesome. You have to try this; I eat it while reading and looking out over the Marina.

In between bites I read and have read Robby's biography over the last couple of days and find it to be an inspiring, eye-opening read. It was very in depth and deep, with a ton of motivation, I am sure Robby and Arden are on with a great seller here as it is very well written and has taken a year or so to produce. I was honoured to be one of the few to read it before it goes to print. The sun shone down on the countless yachts bobbing up and down in the gentle breeze. The water clipped at the side's harbour – yep this is the life.

Then I burnt my lip with some egg white.

'Pleasure pain thing'.

The plan tomorrow is for me to train. I haven't planned to train with Robby again now, but I thought I would head down to Gold's for a quick workout and a study up on what's out there in equipment. So that's what I will do in the morning and then I'll meet with Robby and Arden in the afternoon.

Day 6

I got up early and had my supplements and green tea, showered and shaved and had a breakfast in my room of oats and protein with a black coffee. I then set off walking to Gold's. I walk along the beachfront then head inland a couple of blocks and I am there. I have been here a couple of times before so I enjoy the walk, taking in all the sites down there on the beach.

Gold's

Gold's is, as you would expect, huge with every piece of kit you could ever imagine. I spent a little time looking around at what's out there now for kit and watching people, then I got down to some training.

Shoulders and Arms

I did a similar workout to what I had done with Robby a few days before, but this time I worked my shoulders all at once then moved on to my arms. I did Standing Press, Lat Raise, Bent over Lat Raise for 3 rounds adding weight on each round for 10-12- 8-reps. Yep- all this kit around me and I used a barbell and two dumbbells. For arms I combined Curls with Close Grip Bench Press for 2 rounds, 10 reps each.

Next up, I combined Pushdowns and Cable Curls for 2 rounds. I finished arms with Rope Extensions. I wrapped up the workout with some ab work.

After a great workout there needs to be good food, Robby's base is built on this. There are some awesome bodybuilders out here and they are not the pro's I am talking about. The Joe average out here is way above the Joe average at home. I am convinced it's the working environment and the foods that are available.

So I headed to The Firehouse again, my choice for breakfast number two was egg whites and multigrain pancakes with blueberries. Wow they eat a lot out here and it was huge. I took my time with it, all the while doing the who's who of bodybuilding heading in the door.

Later Robby and Arden picked me up and we headed to Santa Monica for some more filming. This was a great experience as Robby pointed out where he used to live and train and eat in the old days. The interview was fantastic; we talked about all aspects of our sport for at least 45 minutes putting tons of information in there for the viewer. After lunch we parted ways and I came down to the beach to write and read, oooh what a life, work, work, work- ha-ha.

Day 6 – Homeward Bound

The last day of a fantastic week. I headed over to the Marina Café below the gym in the morning and had my last Lou's Special. Whilst waiting for that to be made I rang home and disrupted the kids watching a movie, glad to see they were missing me. I spoke to Molly and it was all the one word answers "yep, erm, yer, umm".

"Have you missed your Dad babe?" "Yep."

"Ok then, put your Mum on."

After breakfast I read a little of a book that I can highly recommend, a book that Robby gave me called Beyond The Game. It's the collective sports writing of Gary Smith. I will cover it further in my News and Views next month, a great book. I headed down to the beachfront at lunchtime and walked the beach side path towards The Firehouse for my last lunch. With this being a Sunday the front was packed out with people.

Once at The Firehouse there were many more characters of the bodybuilding kind this time. I ordered Buffalo- again (ok I like it), egg whites and steamed vegetables; along with this I had wholegrain toast and a coffee. From my seat I could people watch all around me. Two guys were sat over to my left and slightly behind me. They were definitely bodybuilders, one was muscular and the other was on the smooth side.

When they stood up they both puffed up to twice their size and walked to the pay desk with their arms stuck out- I am sure they wanted me to look at them so I did what I normally do which was act unimpressed, I looked everywhere but at them. I could see them but they wouldn't have known. They were doing full body poses just paying the bill. I cannot do with guys like this; they give bodybuilding a bad name. Come on, there is a place for posing and it's not at a pay desk!

After lunch, I headed back to my hotel and packed for home. Robby and Arden picked me up at 3pm to take me to the airport. Get this, Arden gave me a couple of scarves for Louise that she makes and designs. Many celebs out here own her work, so I was honored. Robby gave me some 'Built' baseball caps and had made me a meal for later- Salmon and potatoes, cooked a special way that was delicious. We hugged and said our goodbyes. Waving them off I thought to myself "Wow, Robby Robinson – The Black Prince, one of the greatest bodybuilders to ever live, made my lunch!

Looking over the week, I can say with all certainty that I have had one of the times of my life. If I were never to come back here, I would remember this week with fondness forever. I have learnt a lot- I have been motivated, empowered and inspired beyond words. It is like I have gone full circle.

This very morning before departing for home I sat in the Marina Café and listened to the seagulls. It took me back to my youth growing up in Bridlington, a far cry from LA I know but don't seagulls sound the same all over the world? The days when I was a kid, I would spend down at the waterfront. On one such day I went searching for a Muscle Mag in the local newsagents. I found one and opened it up to see a page with the heading 'Welcome to my World' with a picture of this awesome black bodybuilder- his name was Robby Robinson.

Thank you Robby and Arden, for letting me in to your world.

End Note

I have since this article spent time with Robby a couple more times. A few months ago he was a guest at our home and we ate and trained together for over two week. He also spent time and trained with my 14-year-old son Louis. Can you imagine that at 14!! —I would have given all I had at that age for that opportunity.

I would highly recommend anything Robby produces –his book is the best bodybuilding biography I have ever read and his master class is beyond good –its otherworldly x

Baselines of training and food 2008/2009

I was getting to the point age wise where I could tell things were different – recovery and so on, so I sought the help of Robby taking part in one of his master plan weeks, we were only supposed to spend three days together, but we hit it off so well we spent the whole week training and eating. I am proud to say we still contact each other to this day, in fact Robby text me at 03:00 this morning, still not used to the time difference ha-ha.

To cut a long story short, I learnt a hell of a lot. I was well and truly schooled. Not only that but I got to hear first-hand some incredible stories from the golden era of bodybuilding, while visiting the sites around Santa Monica.

From that year on I started to squeeze every rep as Robby had instructed I learnt so many little tricks of the trade – if you will it was like I had just started working out and had never "really" trained at all. I am telling you in a week I looked better.

Training

Robby influenced after 2008. I finished up that year and started my prep for the May Guest Pose in 2009. For the main part I followed Cheat and Back, Shoulders and Arms, and Legs over my normal Tuesday, Thursday, Saturday schedule, about nine sets per major body part and 6 for smaller areas.

The difference was the style of movement, that I still do now.

I start this diary for you three weeks out from mentioned Guest Pose, as this is the most comprehensive part – I follow my normal programme, with only slight changes to the format – because I was fitting in with Robby at the tail end of my prep as he and Arden came over to spend time with my family and also make an appearance at the Yorkshire.

So again we spent a week together, about two years ago Robby was in the UK again and he spent two weeks with me and Louis. I made just about every meal for him during that time so I know exactly how he eats, day in day out, which brings me to food.

Nutrition

Here again a huge learning curve – I adapted many of Robby's eating ideas from late 2008 – through till a few weeks out from the guest spot, and from that point on it has never really gone back to the old way.

Let me explain.

Robby's eating plan

1   Eggs and beef or Turkey, bread, nut butter

2   Post workout – apple juice, protein powder

3   Beef or turkey, eggs, oats - steel cut

4   Nuts and fruit

5   Chicken thighs, Jasmin rice, veg

6   Nuts and fruit

7   Chicken, Turkey or fish, potatoes and veg

I tried to eat very similar but really struggled with digestion of the meat sources of protein. This only started happening around 2007 – 2008, I realised my digestive system was kicking back with all the years of eating to balance my training.

Also in early 2008 I experimented with a new type diet and had some Pemmican, this gave me a parasite that took months to get rid of.

I tried everything but eventually found a company in the USA that did an all-natural herb formula that eventually killed it off. I would not wish that on my worst enemy.

For all learnt from Robby, I also learnt to listen to my own body and digestive system. Eventually I reduced protein down to barely anything and ate mainly eggs and nuts, I kept trying though, over the next few weeks until eventually I hardly ever ate meat, and I still don't to this day. Let me also add that in all the years I have trained and competed, say 43 years of training, 35 of them on stage I would say, 17 to 20 of these I was ovo lacto vegetarian and it was never a detriment to me at all I still won shows.

But looking back I felt healthy, very healthy, today I eat meat only a few times a week, as you know my diet is based on eggs, yogurt, fruit, veg and lots of healthy carbs. Each to their own.

Supplements

I learnt from Robby the awesome properties of BCAA, Glutamine and Creatine.

Robby had me having BCAA 45 minutes after each meal and half an hour before a meal some creatine and glutamine.

So you ate a meal say 07:00, 07:45 have BCAA, wait until 30 minutes before your next meal and have creatine and glutamine. Basically taking BCAA Glutamine and Creatine between meals.

So in a nutshell, 45 minutes after a meal have BCAA, then 30 minutes before your next meal have creatine and glutamine. Creatine and glutamine looks a faff-about but it is highly effective. This I might add was done on non-training days, rest days. Now I said to Robby - why do you not do this on a training day? His reply was that non training days you need the recovery and repair. This ensures optimum recovery. Training days -you have BCAA, creatine, glutamine, first thing and last thing, morning and evening, and just after your workout in a post-workout drink.

This made a huge transformation in my body – fullness and condition was unreal. I have never forgot the importance of BCAA since. BCAA – lowers oestrogen and stops the body tapping into muscle cells to absorb the BCAA it needs under stress.

For many years I have seen similar results in my clients.

Wrap up

All in all a very good few years of learning, I understood better how to train to target muscle. I understood the importance of eating in a way that works with your system.

I understood the value of supplements for the natural bodybuilder and how best to take them, enjoy these entries.

Saturday 9 May 2009, supplements all bang on

05:00 up (lie in ha-ha)

Egg whites and oats, peanut butter (490)

Post workout (196) Oil (100) Flax – rice cakes (200)

6oz turkey (300) Spud (200) and Veg (75) peanut butter (100)

Pro mix (200)

Chicken salad (250) (100) pasta (100)

Egg whites peanut butter (190)

(2501)

Workout with Vince

Incline press 20kg x 12, 22.5kg x 10, 25kg x 8

*Note – these are listed as weights on each side of the bar

Dumbbell press floor 22.5kg x 12, 25kg x 10, 30kg x 6

Flyes 20kg x 12, 22.5kg x 10, 22.5 x 10

T Bar 2 plates x 12, 2 plates + 5kg x 10, + 2 ½ x 6

Chins 12 – 10 – 8

Dumbbell rows 2 x 10

Calves toe press 3 x 20

Sunday 10 May 2009

1   Up, morning supplements (creatine glutamine and BCAA as well)

     3oz Oats, 6 egg whites, 1 peanut butter (450) (meal 1 supplements)

     45 minutes BCAA

     30 minutes before next meal creatine and glutamine and water

2   Pro with herbs (225) (meal 2 sups) if lunch or meal 3

     45 minutes 5 BCAA

     30 minutes before next meal creatine and glutamine and water

3   6oz Turkey (300) green beans (50) spud (200) peanut butter (100) (meal 2 sups)

     45 mins 5 BCAA

     30 minutes before next meal creatine glutamine and water

4   Pro (225)

     45 mins BCAA

     30 minutes after creatine and glutamine

5   Beef 6oz (300) veg (75) peanut butter (100) (meal 3 sups)

45 mins BCAA

30 minutes creatine and glutamine

6   Egg whites and peanut butter (190)

(2215)

Monday 11 May 2009

Sups

1   Oats and pro, 1 peanut butter (490) (sups)

45 mins BCAA

30 minutes before creatine and glutamine all day through)

2   Pro and herbs (225)

3   Beef (300) green beans (50) spud (200) peanut (100) (sups)

4   Pro (225)

5   Chicken (250) veg (75) peanut (100)

Bed sups

(2015)

Tuesday 12 May 2009

Sups

1   Oats 3oz, 1 scoop pro, 1 peanut butter (490) (sups)

2   Coffee and pro, workout sups

3   Post workout (196) rice cakes (200)

4   Chicken (250) spud (200) veg (50) Peanut (100)

5   Pro (225)

6   Pro after workout two whey and flax oil (200)

7   Chicken (250) veg (75) Peanut (100)

8   Egg whites x 6 peanut butter (190)

(2526)

Workout 1 Chest and back

Dumbbell incline press 22.5kg x 12, 27.5kg x 10, 30kg x 6

Flat D press 22.5kg x 12, 27.5kg x 10, 30kg x 6

Flat flyes 17.5kg 3 x 12

Bent over rows 20kg 3 x 10-12

Chins 10 – 8 – 6 Behind neck and slow and squeeze

Low rows 3 sets 9 plates x 12, 10 plates x 10, 11 plates x 8

Hypers 3 x 10

Abs 6 sets

Workout 2 in early evening at home

Lunges thick bar 3 x 10

Squats thick bar 3 x 15

Sissy squats 7 x 10

Wednesday 13 May 2009

1   Oats 3oz 6 egg whites 1 peanut butter (490) (sups)

        BCAA 45 minutes creatine and glutamine 30 minutes – same as always off day training

        This has worked awesome (look mega)

2   Pro, herbs (225)

        Sups

3   Chicken (350) spud (200) veg (50)

        45 minutes sups

4   Chicken (250) veg (75) peanut butter (100)

5   Egg whites x 6 peanut butter (190)

        Sups

        1930

        Low today, as I had a visit from LA – Jim Tally and Mercedes, awesome couple.

        Look absolutely shredded – freaky ripped

Thursday 14 May 2009

        Sups

1   3oz oats and whey, 1 peanut butter (490) sups – carbs 45

        Pre workout sups. These were odd times Vit E and B it added to a huge pump.

        Workout

        Shoulders and arms did with Jon, front and rear press, DB lat raise and bent over lat raise 3 rounds

        Curls and seated curls 3 rounds

        Extensions and close grip press same bar 3 rounds

2   Post workout (196) rice cakes (200) carbs – 60

3   6oz turkey (300) sweet potatoes (200 Veg (75) peanut butter (100) sups – carbs 50

4   After another workout at home calves and abs

Roman chair sit ups and standing one dumbbell calf raise 5 sets

Seated calf raises and leg tucks 3 sets

Pro whey, creatine BCAA and glutamine (100)

5   Turkey (300) veg (75) peanut butter (100) – 6oz of cooked weight turkey - carbs 20

6   3oz of cooked weight turkey, a bit of salad (150) (50) cider vinegar – carbs 10

2336

Carbs 185

Training day

Friday 15 May 2009

Sups

1   Oats 3oz and whey and peanut butter (490)

45 mins aminos BCAA (glutamine 30 minutes before creatine)

2   Pro (225)

45 mins BCAA

30 minutes as normal

3   Turkey (300) Spud (200) Veg (50) peanut butter (100)

Same – BCAA etc

Same

4   Pro (225)

Same

Same

5   Chicken (250) veg (75) peanut butter (100)

6   Some almonds (150) a bit of melon

2165

135 carbs

Saturday 16 May 2009, start new diet 2 weeks to go

Feel bunged up need to detox a bit, and clean up my foods even more – carbs need to go up a little now also, as I am shredded

Based on Andreas Cahling – adding fruits before and after workout

Water, Vit C Creatine – morning supplements

Banana and some grapes (200)

1   30 minutes on hour (180) 2 eggs 2 oz of oats (180) sups

Pre workout sups

Workout

Leg extensions 2 sets

Leg curls 2 sets

Leg press 2 sets

Squats 2 sets

Stiff leg 2 sets

Walking lunge 2 sets

Killer workout

Post workout

2   Grapes and banana (200) creatine and glutamine, BCAA

09:30 Aminos BCAA and glutamine

3   Salad (50) 1oz brazil nuts (170) egg (90) spud (200)

Afternoon (Aminos BCAA) and glutamine

4   Veg (75) 2 eggs (180)

5   Nuts 1oz or so (150) some melon (50)

1725 – 160 carbs

Extra chest at 18:00 in garage, and a bit of back and calves

Sunday 17 May 2009, up carbs

Notes – look absolutely awesome on this eating plan, loo was back to normal today, I have struggled for weeks months even to be okay (normal)

Condition today was mega sharp striations in places I have never had them just all I need to do now is eat up a little now, add up carbs.

First thing supplements – creatine glutamine BCAA and Robby's baseline.

30 minutes grapes 3oz (100) – carbs 10

1   2 eggs (180) 2oz of oats (180) banana (100) (sups) – carbs 50

45 minutes BCAA

30 minutes before next meal creatine and glutamine

2   1oz oats (90) spud pumpkin seeds (150) whey (100) – carbs 45

45 minutes BCAA

30 minutes before creatine and glutamine

3   1oz nuts almonds (160) egg (90) 250g sweet pot (250) veg (75) – carbs 55, 15

45 minutes BCAA

30 minutes creatine and glutamine

4   Veg a lot (100) 2 poached eggs (180), carbs – 20

5   Nuts 1oz (150) melon 100g (50, carbs 10

Felt a little tired today but look awesome and feel good on this eating plan

1955

205 carbs

Note – baseline supplements were Vitamin C, Vitamin D, B-complex with main meals. Sometimes before workouts B-complex and Vitamin E for huge pump, did this a few times on chest days.

Monday 18 May 2009

Carbs up and calories a little again and move up over the next few weeks

1   Aminos creatine glutamine and morning sups, 3oz of grapes (150) carbs 10

2   Breakfast 2 eggs (180) 3 oz of oats (270) banana on top (100) carbs 76

45 mins BCAA

30 mins before next meal creatine and glutamine

3   1oz nuts almonds (160) 1 egg (90) 250g of sweet pot (260) veg (75) carbs 70

45 mins BCAA

30 minutes creatine and glutamine

4   1 scoop whey (100) in 1oz seeds (150) 1oz oats (90) carbs 17

45 mins BCAA

30 mins normal again

5   Veg lots (100) 2 poached eggs (190) tea carbs 20

6   1oz nuts (150) 100g of melon (50) carbs 10

2115

203 – this will be cool for this week see how I look

Tuesday 19 May 2009

Sum up – after training look very very good

Condition is scary – absolutely shredded Chris called me a shredded wheat

Diet is working

Workout

Incline press bar 20kg x 12, 22.5kg x 8, 25kg x 6

Flat dumbbell press 22.5kg x 12, 27.5kg x 8, 27.5kg x 6

Flat flyes 17.5kg 3 x 12

Back

T bar 2 plates x 12, 2.5 x 10, 2.5 + 5kg x 6

Chins 3 x 8 – 10, behind neck

Low rows 3 x 10 – 12

Abs 6 sets

Later in day cable crunch, leg tucks, and calves toe press 3 rounds

Posed two rounds

Sups

1   Fruit (50) melon +, carbs 10

2	2 eggs (180) oats 3oz (270) banana (100) carbs 76
3	Fruit post workout (150) carbs 25
4	1 scoop whey (100) 1 oz oats (90) 1oz seeds (150) carbs 17
5	Lunch – 1 egg (90) nuts (160) 200g potatoes (200) veg (75) carbs 60
6	Veg (100) 2 eggs (180) carbs 20
7	Nuts (150) 100g melon (50) carbs 10

2095, carbs 218

Chilled at night watched film

Ready for big day week

Wednesday 20 May 2009, busy day, rest day training

| 1 | Sups and fruit (50) carbs 10 |
| 2 | 2 eggs (180) oats 3oz (270) banana (100) carbs 76 |

45 mins BCAA

30 mins before next meal creatine and glutamine

| 3 | 1oz seeds (150) whey (100) oats 1oz (90) carbs 17 |

45 mins BCAA

30 mins before creatine and glutamine

| 4 | 1oz almonds (160) egg (90) 250g sweet potatoes (260) veg (50) carbs 70 |

45 mins BCAA

30 minutes creatine and glutamine

| 5 | Veg (100) 2 poached eggs (190), carbs 20 |
| 6 | 1oz nuts melon (150) (50) carbs 10 |

1990

203 carbs

Thursday 21 May 2009, training day

Got Robby DVD today – bloody awesome

| 1 | Fruit and sups – 100g (50) melon, carbs 10 |

2 eggs (180) oats 3oz (270) banana (100) sups, carbs 76

2	Seeds (150) Whey (100) Oats (90) carbs 17
3	Eggs (90) 1oz nuts (160) sweet potatoes 250g (260) veg (50) carbs 70
4	BCAA glutamine
5	2 eggs (190) veg (100) carbs 25
6	1oz nuts melon (150) (50) carbs 10

Added ½ tuna (100) salad (50) few more grapes (50) carbs 20

2190, carbs 228

Busy day still - good

Louise said I looked a little flat so eat more at supper

Legs

3 sets of front squats

Leg press 3 sets

Leg extensions 3 sets

Leg curl 3 sets

Calf raise 3 sets

Seated calf raise 3 sets

Abs roman chair 3 sets

Crunches 3 sets

Practiced posing and had a little bike ride with kids

Friday 22 May 2009, busy day today

1   2 eggs (180) 3oz oats (270) banana (100), carbs 76

      45 mins – then 30 mins as normal

2   Nuts 1oz seeds (160) whey (100) oats (90), carbs 17

      45 mins and 30 mins as normal

3   250g Sweet potato (260) tuna (100) veg (75) flax (100), carbs 70

      45 mins and 30 mins as normal

4   2 eggs (190) veg (100), carbs 20

6   Turkey (90) Salad (75), carbs 10

      Supplements are all bang on to the plan Robby sent me

      1oz rice cake (93), carbs 19

      1983

      212 carbs

Saturday 23 May 2009, training day

Look absolutely super shredded – never looked this good, stick to the plan, its killing me but stick with it

1   Eggs (180) 3oz oats (270) Banana (100) sups, carbs 76

      Pre workout supplements

      Workout

      Incline dumbbell press 3 sets

Flat dumbbell press 3 sets

Flyes 3 sets

Bent over rows 3 sets

Chins behind neck 3 sets

Pullovers 3 sets

Shrugs 3 sets

Fruit (120), carbs 25

2   1oz oats (90) seeds 1oz (150) whey (100), carbs 17

3   250g sweet potato (260) eggs (90) nuts (100) salad (50), carbs 65

4   Veg (100) 2 eggs (190), carbs 20

5   Tuna (100) salad (75) nuts (160), carbs 10

Carbs 213

Calories 2135

Bike ride late with Louis, got calves – practiced posing as normal

Had a walk around the park with the kids – cannot sit still

Sunday 24 May 2009

Sups morning – as Robby's way as normal

1   2 eggs (190) 3oz oats (270) banana (100) sups, carbs 76

45 mins BCAA

30 mins creatine glutamine

2   1 oz Seeds (150) whey (100) 1oz oats (90), carbs 17

45 mins – BCAA

30 mins creatine and glutamine

3   Salad (75) egg (90) almonds (160) 1oz rice cakes (93), carbs 29

45 mins BCAA

30 mins later creatine and glutamine

4   2 eggs (190) veg (75), carbs 20

45 mins BCAA

30 mins before next – creatine and glutamine

5   Salad (75) tuna (100) nuts (160), carbs 10

1918 – low

Carbs 152

Sun was out today – relaxed a bit

Bike and later with Louise and practised my posing

Monday 25 May 2009, bank holiday, training day

Picking Robby and Arden up, daft sod tomorrow

Morning sups – as Robby's

1. 2 eggs (190) 3 oats (270) banana (100) sups, carbs 76
2. 1oz seeds (150) whey (100) oats (90), carbs 17
3. Salad (25) egg (90) almonds (160) 1oz rice cake (93), carbs 29

Workout pre-workout sups

Workout at Village – a little extra legs also (walked there and back)

Leg extensions 3 sets

Leg curls, 3 sets

Lunges 2 sets

Leg press 3 sets

Lat raise calf 3 sets

Seated lat raise 3 sets

Bent over lat raise 3 sets

Standing press 3 sets

Overhead triceps extensions rope 3 sets

Close grip press 3 sets

Single arm pushdowns 3 sets

Curls 3 sets

Concentration curls 3 sets

Cable 3 sets

Abs – rope crunch – toe press 3 sets

Hanging leg raise – toe press 3 sets

Fruit (120), carbs 25

Creatine and glutamine BCAA

4. Veg (75) eggs x 2 (190) rice cakes (93), carbs 39
5. Salad (75) Tuna (100) nuts (160), carbs 10

2081

Carbs 196

Tuesday 26 May 2009

Picking Robby up again got the flights mixed up yesterday!

Up – sups

1   2 eggs (190) 3oz oats (270) banana (100) sups, carbs 70

Had a really good day yesterday felt like a pro bodybuilder – meals on time and training and doing posing and the like. Enjoy this week. I will look back on this in years and remember this week with Robby and the show

Robby eats

1 – 2 yolks, 4 eggs all together 4oz beef or turkey, 3 ¼ cup oats, bread – almond butter

2 – Same, bread, almond butter

3 – Beef – or chicken, or turkey, veg, spuds or rice

4 – Rice cakes original creatine glutamine aminos or pro

5 – Fish, veg, once a week (pasta day before legs)

Speaking at Frankie & Bennies

Just as snacks early in day – banana apples

Eats beef mainly before leg day

2   Salad (75) egg (90) nuts (100) 1oz rice cakes (93), carbs 29

3   Fruit after workout (120) carbs 25

Workout with Robby

Flat bench press dumbbell 7 – 7 – 7 adding up

Flat flyes 7 – 7 – 7 adding up

Low rows 3 sets adding up 12 – 10 – 8

Pulldown 7 – 7 – 7 1 set, 2 x 8 then front and back

Vacuum pose 3 sets of 10 with 5 mins walk on treadmill

Bike with Louis later in evening

4   2 eggs (190) veg (75) rice cakes (93), carbs 29

5   Tuna (100) salad (50) small nuts (160), carbs 10

1706 too low

Carbs 163

Wednesday 27 May 2009, up early work until lunch, meet Robby again

Up very early 3ish

Had breakfast at 4ish, morning sups

1   2 eggs (190) 3oz oats (270) banana (100) sups, carbs 76

2   1oz oats (90) seeds 1oz (150) veg (100), carbs 17

Pre workout sups, plus add in some extra creatine before and after also some glutamine. This will give me a workout – energy rush – have a coffee also

3   Fruit with creatine after and BCAA and glutamine, fruit (120), carbs 20

4   1 egg (98) nuts (160) salad (75) sweet potato 250g (260), carbs 70

5   130g raw weight turkey (190) veg (75), carbs 20

6   Same as 5, carbs 20

2143

Carbs 223

Workout Robby

Curls 3 sets 7 – 7 – 7 adding up

Cable curls 10 – 10 – 10 adding up

Shoulder press machine 7 – 7 – 7 adding up, and with forced reps cable, lat raise side and rear 3 sets

Workout later on in yard

Lunges 3 sets, stiff leg dumbbell 3 sets (done)

Going into turkey tonight, lower in sodium and more sustaining for me now feel good but a little fatigued

Up carbs from tomorrow and BCAA and glutamine and creatine the off days just pose tomorrow and light pump

Look absolutely awesome, so happy, full and shredded

Thursday 28 May 2009, start to up carbs a bit and calories from today, small piece of turkey will be around 250 - 300

1   Eggs (190) 3oz oats (270) banana (100), carbs 76

45 mins BCAA

30 mins before next meal

2   1oz oats (90) 1oz seeds (150) 1 scoop whey (100), carbs 17

45 mins – then 30 mins creatine and glutamine

3   Turkey (140) 200g sweet potato (200) veg (75) cider vinegar, carbs 55

Same with supplements again

4   Turkey (140) 200g sweet potato (200) veg (50) cider vinegar, carbs 55

Sups as same – 45 – and 30 mins before

5   Turkey (140) salad (50), carbs 10

1895 fats gone down a little

Carbs up, 213

This should be fine approximately 50g more than I have been on, see how I look

Started emptying BCAA capsules out into a scoop and swilling them down now

Still 3 litre of water

Friday 29 May 2009

Reduce seeds now and do two oat meals

½ a banana in each, 2 x 2oz oat meals, 1 egg each also

This will split up the carbs and keep waist small

1   1 egg (90) oats (180) half banana, carbs 44

45 mins – aminos and creatine as normal

2   1 egg (90) oats (180) half banana, carbs 44

Same sups

3   Turkey (140) 200g sweet potato (200) veg or salad (50) cider vinegar, carbs 55

45 mins sups

30 mins before next – creatine and glutamine

4   Turkey (140) veg (75) 1oz rice cake (93), carbs 29

5   Salad (75) turkey (140), carbs 10

1453

Carbs 182

Go for 180g of carbs reduced slightly from yesterday felt really full, muscles bursting

2 litres of water

Saturday 30 May 2009

Sups

1   1 egg (90) steel cut oats (180) half banana sups (50), carbs 44

45 mins and 30 mins sups

2   Same as 1, carbs 44

Same sups as 1

3   Turkey (140) 200g sweet potato (200) veg and salad (50) sups, carbs 50

45 mins and 30 mins sups

4   Filet steak (300) 200g potato (200) veg (75), carbs 55

45 mins and 30 mins

5   Turkey (140) salad (75) wine 1 glass red all night, carbs 10

1820

Carbs 213 fine

2 litre of water 180g carbs and a glass of wine, melon also

More cals, have a steak at night

Spent lots of time with Arden and Robby

Sunday 31 May 2009, todays the day

Sups

1   (up at 4am) 3 eggs (270) almonds (100), steel cut oats (180) half banana (50), carbs 44

2   8ish steel cut oats (180) half banana (50) a few more flaked almonds (50), carbs 44

3   Had a meal turkey spud and salad

Flap jack back stage and wine

Looked best ever, everybody said I was

Cheat later – steak veg spud ice cream, small bowl of cornflakes, cake 2 pieces, bit of chocolate. Not too much.

Photos by Eric Guy

Last set together

I hope you enjoyed this book.

Brought to you from the pages of my journals that have seen so many workouts and good food whilst in front of me. Either lifting the iron or tucking into a meal.

One workout at a time, one meal at a time, each week ticked off with a goal in mind.

Putting your thoughts on paper the old school way, transfers that thought into something real. There to prompt you, urge you, and encourage you.

If I can give you some parting words, they would be…

Be the best you can be. Always strive towards your goals whatever they may be. Also, document everything, because in the years to come you will look back and be so proud of your accomplishments.

Thank you for your trust and thank you for buying my book.

Love to all.

Ian xx

About the author

Ian Duckett is a natural for life bodybuilder, having won British, European, Pro-Am and World titles, throughout his career of 40 years.

Ian resides in Leeds with his two children, Molly and Louis, and now partner Jo. Dedicated still to a life of health and fitness and helping others achieve the same.

www.oldbutstrong.co.uk

ian@oldbutstrong.co.uk

Follow Ian on Instagram @oldbutstrong

Ian Duckett

Author of:

Short and Sharp
True Grit
Old But Strong
Natural Progression
and many more

brings you another sure-fire best seller

Old But Strong The Journals brings you Ian's personal journals in a book packed with information from the health and strength enthusiast to the competitive natural bodybuilder at any level

Made in United States
Troutdale, OR
01/03/2024

16649658R00117